Darwin or Design?
What Biology Reveals
About the Secrets of Life

Darwin or Design?
What Biology Reveals
About the Secrets of Life

INTELLIGENT DESIGN
INTRODUCTORY GUIDE

Scott S. Chandler

Lecture Press

DARWIN OR DESIGN?
What Biology Reveals about the Secrets of Life

1. Non-fiction- 2. Science- 3. Apologetics- 4. Biology

ISBN-10: 0692820973

EAN- 13: 9780692820971

Library of Congress Control Number: 2016918604
Lecture Press, Dallas, TX

First published in the United States by Lecture Press, Dallas, TX

Printed in the United States of America

To:

My wife Pamela

The legacy of my grandparents Edwin and Sarah, who passed timeless truths to at least one more in the next generation.

Contents

Preface

⟨⟨⟨⟨

IN ITS NASCENT BEGINNINGS, THE age of science began as another way to affirm the varied mysteries of the Creator. But humanity's fascination and idolatry with the material world eclipsed God as a social construct. Western thought replaced Him with a random, naturalistic and purposeless view of the world as descended through a series of secondary causes. As authoritative and relevant literature, the Bible went out of fashion in an increasingly materialistic and rationalistic age. The very philosophies descending from the biblical text, on which much of the Western world was built—a world of purpose, design, and a priori first things, was replaced by a universe characterized by chance and closed-system naturalism. Without correspondence to ultimate reality, academia today is dominated by a theory of life that coheres to reductionism (where all of reality is reduced to materials). If matter is all there is, then matter is all that matters. Physicist Stephen Hawking summarized the emphasis of our times: "The scientific account is complete. Theology is unnecessary" (Hawking 2010).

Though academic atheists believe they have recaptured the intellectual high ground, they haven't thought through the assumptions upon which the theory of evolution sits. Dissecting Darwinism exposes the logical fallacies and contradictions within the theory, where conclusions are built on false assumptions. The issues of contention between evolution and intelligent design are complex and this guide houses some of the best research to introduce the salient issues in the conflicting theories about life's origins. Strained from mounds of material, it presents the concepts in a way that is easier to grasp than many textbooks present, and addresses the philosophical assumptions underwriting modern science. Profitable for private study or for a group/classroom setting, this manual presents objectives before each lesson as well as review questions for discussion. It can also be part of a greater curriculum and supplemented in a course of study with other works on the subject. Blank pages in the back allow for further study of any concept.

Coming to Terms with the Terms in Evolution

———∞∞∞———

OBJECTIVES:

critique the different types of evolution

state the assumptions of Darwin and how the major mechanisms work

distinguish between Darwinists and neo-Darwinists

articulate evidence Darwinists use for supporting their theory.

Icebreaker:

*We are at the dawn of a new era, for we are begin-
ning to recover the knowledge of the external world
that was lost through the fall of Adam. We now observe creatures properly...But by the grace of God we
already recognize in the most delicate flower the won-
ders of divine goodness and omnipotence.*

—Martin Luther

Roman Emperor Marcus Aurelius said that, "He who
does not know what the world is, does not know where he
is, and he who does not know for what purpose the world
exists, does not know who he is, nor what the world is."
Does evolution clarify or confuse an understanding of ourselves and our world? Evolution inundates us from many
angles. We are exposed to the theory early in school and all
of us apprehend it on some level. Even believers raised in
Christian homes or attend Christian schools can be indoc-
trinated from childhood. Evolution oozes from our sub-
conscious and we cannot escape its phrases, concepts and
nomenclature. And it is a notion that shapes our thinking
in areas beyond biology. Political "progressives" believe
mankind gets better through time to the extent humans
parallel the upgrades received from nature. We use a cliché

when we make a mistake, or when we are maturing and say, "I must be evolving." Evolution shapes our thinking, and many Christians stay away from it even as they engage people with the gospel and related subjects such as the purpose of life.

God allows great systems of thought, based on "human teachings" (Col. 2:22), to be built up against Him. Even as we are inundated with inaccurate assumptions in science, evolution can disinterest Christians so much they don't peer into the topic at all. They rightly dismiss it as a heretical deception underwritten by atheistic scientists, turning away from this opposing idea "of what is falsely called knowledge" (1 Tim. 6:20). But they can do so without refutation and little attempt to free those so enslaved by the system. There is deception in its assumptions to be sure, but because it falters under scrutiny evolution doesn't have to cause fear. Even though it is billeted as bedrock truth by academic elites, evolution is still just a theory and an inferior one at that. It is possible the scheme will be sidelined out of favor in mainline science even within a century or so (based on the rate of how many scientists are disavowing the theory). As Malcolm Muggeridge commented, "I, myself, am convinced that the theory of evolution, especially to the extent to which it's been applied, will be one of the great jokes in the history books of the future" (Muggeridge 1980, 59). Far from settled fact, evolution is as much a philosophy of science issue as it is about raw naked data, as much about interpretation as observation. Therefore, we probe it because, as C.S. Lewis said, "bad philosophy needs to be answered" (Lewis 1980, 28).

Evolution is a general term most often pertaining to biology and carries secular connotations. But biological evolution actually has three components that, when understood, exposes some of its intricate deceptions. First, there is *microevolution* where organisms exhibit limited differences over time through adaptation to changing environments, or where gene expressions can vary from an established preexisting code. Bacteria developing resistance to certain antibiotics is an example of microevolution. The term *survival of the fittest*, or where "nature don't take too kindly to wimps" (as one expert paraphrases it), pertains to this branch of evolution. Sometimes known as *small scale-evolution*, microevolution is an observed reality and has elements that do not necessarily threaten a creationist worldview.

Next, is *macroevolution* where organisms larger than species have evolved from a common ancestor. That is, everything higher than a species on the taxonomic chart is said to evolve, such as genus, family, order, class, phylum, and kingdom. From here the great "tree of life" is presented, where everything that exists can theoretically be traced to a common ancestor. The trunk represents the common ancestor and the ends of the branches symbolize the evolved living organisms. The last category of evolution is *chemical evolution* where scientific naturalists, by necessity, attempt to address origins and "the arrival of the fittest." Here, life supposedly began by a spontaneous collision of molecules through self-organization in a warm, watery environment.

Some evolutionists blame creationists or design advocates with an unnecessary partition of the three branches of evolution. When Darwinists say they believe in evolution, often they are referring to macroevolution because the segmentation of the three branches exposes the weaknesses of the whole propoundment. The problem with blaming creationists for this tripartite division is that the term "microevolution" itself was coined by a neo-Darwinist in the twentieth century. And it was Russian biochemist, Alexander Oparin, who proposed an entirely materialistic hypothesis for the origin of life in chemical evolution; his theory left terms in our modern vernacular such as "sea of chemicals" and "prebiotic soup." Based on closed system naturalism, he held that simple chemicals formed organic compounds, which in turn constructed large, complex molecules such as proteins that somehow remained interconnected inside a cell wall.

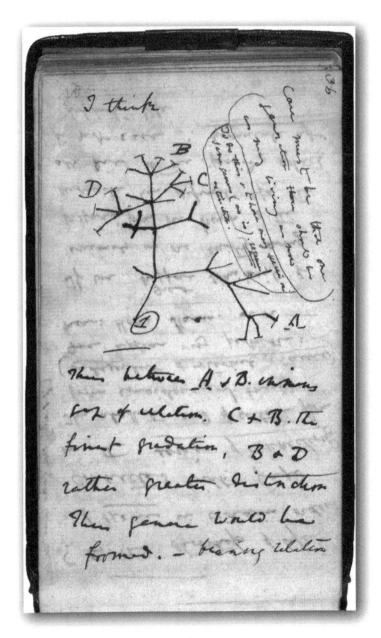

With the words "I think" at the top, Charles Darwin drew this early sketch of the Tree of Life in a notebook dated to 1837, after his return from the Galapagos Islands on the HMS Beagle (Darwin, 1837). Darwin was not the first to propose such a tree. In the 3rd century, Neo-platonist philosopher Porphyry arranged Aristotle's categories of species into a tree, and wondered whether they were "pure isolated conceptions." In addition, the "transmutation of species" had already been in the public consciousness from earlier writings such as that of French naturalist Jean Baptiste Lamarck. And millennia earlier, Aristotle held that "Nature proceeds little by little from things lifeless to animal life in such a way that it is impossible to determine the exact line of demarcation."

Darwin's grandfather Erasmus furthered the idea of a transmutation of species years before Darwin's landmark book, even though he retained some theistic notions. Departing from the distinct "kinds" at the moments of creation and distorting the singular source of life's origins, Erasmus wrote: "imagine that all warm-blooded animals have arisen from one living filament...with the power of acquiring new parts...and of delivering down these improvements by generation to its posterity" (Darwin 1818, 397).

The notes on this page from Darwin's notebook read, from top to bottom, "I think ... Case must be that one generation then should be as many living as now. To do this and to have many species in same genus (as is) requires extinction. Thus between A & B immense gap of relation. C & B the finest gradation, B & D rather greater distinction. Thus genera would be formed.—bearing relation." Darwin would later write in On the Origin of Species that, "The affinities of all the beings of the same class have sometimes been represented by a great tree. I believe this simile largely speaks the truth. The green and budding twigs may represent existing species; and those produced during each former year may represent the long succession of extinct species" (Darwin 1859, Chapter 4).

What has biology revealed about a tree in the years since Darwin? Eric Bapteste, an evolutionary biologist at the Pierre and Marie Curie University in Paris, observes that "We have no evidence at all that the tree of life is a reality" (Bapteste, Lawton 2009). At best, the tree is an oversimplification as genes are not merely passed down to individual branches. Some have called the tree an "impenetrable thicket" and Darwin elsewhere said it may be a "tangled bank." Concludes Michael Rose, an evolutionary biologist at the University of California, Irvine, "The tree of life is being politely buried...What's less accepted is that our whole fundamental view of biology needs to change" (Rose, Sample 2009). Though we are built to categorize the material world by similar elements, analogous characteristics in no way guarantee biological descent but could easily mean shared design.

In the mid-1800s, Darwin originally theorized a tree of life from his studies of breeding as well as from fossils. Though he never saw any transitions, he *speculated* that there must be sophisticated and complex links in the lineage of creatures and among species. The major groups of life should blend smoothly and seamlessly into one another through countless transitional forms (Dembski and Wells 2008, 60). Darwin did not know about genetics nor could he have anticipated the problem information would bear on a naturalistic theory for origins. But he did believe there was some inward process in organisms that caused the changes, as opposed to the view of a predecessor where mere external pressures from the environment elicited changes.

That inward process has now become more refined. What originally started as a theory based on morphological and structural similarities in animal features, is carried forward by neo-Darwinists to the inner workings of the cell in justifying the assumptions. Darwin initially formed his theory from the fossil record and breeding programs. Today, neo-Darwinists carry the torch to vindicate macroevolution through the studies of genetics and molecular biology. What originally began as a theory based on similarity of appearance in basic structures and functions of organisms (morphology), is now brought internally into the realm of biogenetics and the inner workings of the cell to find similarity of appearance of micro systems and validate large-scale evolutionary change. Though neo-Darwinism is mandatory to keep Darwin's theory alive (since evidence for his primal assertions are thin), it too can be considered a dogma hung on assumptions. Evolutionist Richard Milton writes: "neo-Darwinism has ceased to be a scientific theory and has been transformed into an ideology—an overarching belief system that pervades all thinking in the life sciences and beyond" (Milton 1997, 240).

MIDPOINT QUESTIONS:

Is evolution something to be feared or should it be scrutinized?

What are the different types of evolution?

Is there a form of "evolution" creationists agree with?

What is chemical evolution and what terms do we get from it?

What is the history of the "tree-of-life" and what is its status today?

University of Chicago evolutionary geneticist Jerry Coyne supplies a definition of evolution that holds some uncertainty for a theory presumed as rock-solid science:

"Organisms gradually evolved over time and split into different species, and the main engine of evolutionary change was natural selection. Sure, some details of these processes are unsettled, but there is no argument among biologists about the main claims" (Coyne 2007). We are going to see this is far from the truth, not only that organisms gradually evolved, but that "all" biologists are in agreement as to evolution's main claims.

Within macroevolution are important terms such as "LUCA" and "modification with descent." LUCA refers to the search for the last universal common ancestor, perhaps in the phyla category, to which all living organisms trace their lineage. LUCA may not refer the search for the first organism per se, but the search for the last ancestor from which major groupings of life can theoretically be traced. Even modern forms of Darwin's theory are based on the assumption of common ancestry, or common descent. For the engine of macroevolution to be sustained, modification with descent characterizes the changes taking place within organisms on small incremental levels over time, usually long periods of time. This concept is a major premise of evolution and purports to affirm the basic philosophy of Darwin, where organisms fluidly transpose from simple to complex through gradual changes and the transmutation of species.

The branch of chemical evolution is where life reputedly started by a spontaneous collision of molecules that self-organized in a warm watery environment of elements.

This area of evolution falls under the category of *origin science*, which is a speculative discipline since the past is gone and not currently visible. *Operational science*, which biology falls under, studies processes that occur today. Though the title of Darwin's book is "The Origin of the Species," it has little to do with origins; it is a theory of the morphing of life-forms once they somehow got going. But where did they originally come from? As we will see, that is still the great mystery that confounds biologists.

Darwinism is a generic term from science that refers to the formation of life in a closed system, by mere natural processes. The *two primary mechanisms* of Darwinism are random mutation (or variation by chance) and natural selection. Random chance is the supposed generative force through the mutation of new organisms. Natural selection is the restrictive force that saves or "cuts back" from an existing

pool of organisms that are most adaptive. Throughout this course, Darwinism will refer to the two aspects of evolution, macroevolution and chemical evolution, that characterize scientists who believe life formed and continued in a closed system by natural processes. Both the fossil evidence and/or molecular biology are invoked with varying degrees of emphases to support the theory when it's most expedient.

REVIEW QUESTIONS:

What is chemical evolution and what terms do we get from it?

What are the different branches of evolution?

What are the two main mechanisms of Darwinism?

Who are neo-Darwinists and what assumption do they operate under?

Which two disciplines do Darwinists tap into for support of their theory?

Coming to Terms with the Term of Intelligent Design

—∞∞∞—

OBJECTIVES:

define intelligent design and state what it does and does not do

state the twin pillars of intelligent design

articulate how design cooperates with nature and is distinguished from secondary causes

explain design's great contribution to science and how it contends with a world guided by natural forces

ICEBREAKER:

It is absurd to suppose that purpose is not present because we do not observe the agent deliberating. Art does not deliberate. If the ship-building art were in the wood, it would produce the same results by nature. If, therefore, purpose is present in art, it is present also in nature.

—Aristotle

⸻

"I DO NOT BELIEVE IT is helpful to our students," said presidential candidate Barack Obama, "to cloud discussions of science with non-scientific theories like intelligent design that are not subject to experimental scrutiny" (Obama 2008). Intelligent design as "non-scientific" and "not subject to experimental scrutiny" is propaganda promoted by academic elites who have a preconceived bias against the ramifications of design in reality. The Darwinism Obama has adopted is not so much about science and data as it is an ideology with political motives. If we want to learn about intelligent design and what true science is, we are better served by referring to the scientists who study it. Biochemist Michael Behe says, "The conclusion of intelligent design flows naturally from the data itself—not from sacred books or sectarian beliefs," (Behe 1996).

By definition, intelligent design deconstructs the Darwin delusion and enters the empirical arena as a data borne model; it gains credibility as a first-rate theory by drawing the conclusion of design based on the *indications* of intelligence in nature. As geophysicist Stephen Meyer summarizes, "intelligent design is an evidence-based scientific theory about life's origins that challenges strictly materialistic views of evolution" (Meyer 2009). Intelligent design opposes Darwinism on scientific grounds, and like Darwinism, is a scientific theory. In this guide, design deals with how biological complexity emerged in the history of life.

Specifically, intelligent design does not make inferences as to the nature or attributes of the designer; it merely deals with the artifacts and not the mind of the artifacer.

Despite the accusations of some evolutionary scientists, intelligent design does not make sophisticated theological or metaphysical claims. It may seem incongruent to observe design and not expand on the nature of the designer, but Christian thinkers have been adept in developing the discoveries put forth by intelligent-design scientists in bridging the gap to the existence of the Christian God (see Epilogue). Two pillars of intelligent design, *irreducible complexity* and *specified complexity*, serve to render intelligent causes as empirically detectable and will be studied later. Since science is the process of going from the known to the unknown, design is a logical conclusion and a more cohesive theory than Darwinism about the origin and processes of life. Based on observable data, we have well-defined methods that can distinguish intelligent sources from undirected natural causes.

Midpoint Questions:

What are the two pillars of intelligent design?

How is intelligent design a first-rate theory in the science arena?

How can design be a tool to debunk Darwinism as well as present the greater truths of the faith?

Intelligent design does not eradicate nature nor refute mechanistic processes on every level. Design recognizes, when appropriate, that there are secondary causes in nature as well, such as the difference between an acorn and an oak tree. The two have similarities that correlate, but they are different. The acorn has programmed within it the dynamics necessary to grow into a big tree, and science cannot say it is completely random. It might seem the acorn is guided by some deterministic laws, but it's more logical to argue that an intelligent designer is involved in imparting the necessary information in the acorn.

Design is both anterior to, and complicit with, secondary causes and holds that nature is not the origin of itself

nor manifested by unguided natural forces. The balance of design and natural causes is portrayed by a rusty car sitting in a field. The car shows products of both design (the car) and natural forces (the rust). Blind natural forces, by themselves, could not have produced the design of the car. Likewise, natural forces are not responsible for incredibly complex biomolecular systems. Though intelligent design doesn't make any theological claims specifically, it is worth inserting that Jesus referred to secondary causes as subject to God's sovereignty. For example, he referred to a mustard seed growing to be the biggest tree in the garden (Matt. 13:31–32), or a farmer waiting for his seed to grow. Jeremiah says that God is the source of, and sovereign over, secondary causes like rain: "Do the skies *themselves* send down showers? No, it is you, Lord our God. Therefore our hope is in you, for you are the one who does all this" (Jer. 14:22). Though scientifically useful in categorizing how nature works, thinking only in terms of secondary causes can lead to a dangerous theological middle step in deism. In reality, God is intricately involved and causes all things "to grow" (Col. 2:19). Physical processes are not at odds with God's existence or authorship. But to attribute secondary causes to chance confuses the implements with the implementer.

Intelligent design allows for some naturalistic mechanisms like mutation and natural selection to operate in history, by which organisms are adapted to their environment. But intelligent design holds that nature is

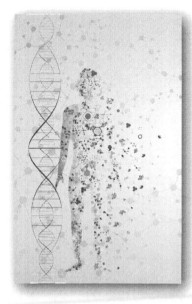

incomplete in possessing all of the resources needed to bring about new biological structures. Nature requires the contribution of design to bring about those formations. Design advocates maintain that the universe we empirically validate, at this moment, is not a closed system where natural causes explain everything. Rather, it is like a wristwatch found in a field with intricate parts of design in operation, to use William Paley's centuries old example. On an empirical level, the physical universe seems to have a designer who interacts with the universe much in the way a skilled musician plays an instrument, even as the instrument itself was caused. Though materials are important, the art of building life exclusively is not in the physical matter that constitutes life. The tangible record evidences design.

Intelligence is particularly displayed in the information-rich biological structures of nature. Because intelligent design is about intelligence, a living organism is not just a clump of matter. What distinguishes organic from inorganic matter is how it is *arranged* with intricate complexity. The dirt under our feet and the matter in our bodies is the same; it is the *arrangement* through information that explains much of the difference. We will discover that naturalistic mechanisms are incapable of producing specific, information-rich structures that make up biology. Since nature displays design that nature alone cannot account for, intelligent design acts in concert with material mechanisms without being reducible to them. As such, miracles (one off events with a specific divine purpose) do not necessarily have to be invoked in the process and physical laws are not inevitably suspended.

Darwinists would rather not acknowledge that divine activity changes the nature of nature. But intelligent design recognizes there are secondary causes in the world, as naturalists hold, whose ultimate origins are identifiable. Though intelligent design is ascribed by more and more scientists as a strict scientific theory, this author believes it is an incongruent to separate design from an accurate and cohesive view of the world. If the God of the Bible created all of visible reality, intelligent design is not metaphysically neutral but correlates perfectly with a true understanding life, origins, purpose, and destiny. Scripture presents sources of information about our world that natural man (guided by a worldview of chance) does not reason to, and each design feature can lead into a presentation of the gospel. The epilogue expands on the nature of the designer by bridging the gap from an intelligent designer to the God of the Bible.

REVIEW QUESTIONS:

Does design eradicate nature? Why or why not?

How does design cooperate with natural causes and where does it differ? What are some examples?

Why do design advocates say the universe is not a closed system?

What role do secondary causes play in the mind of a believer and what is the danger in acknowledging them?

Darwinian Speculation versus Science

———— ❦ ————

OBJECTIVES:

state the two fields Darwinists use to support their theory and when they use them

explain the purposes of science and how Darwinism violates these

outline how Darwinism is more historical novel than reality

ICEBREAKER:

Because of the amount of information available, scientists today are forced into a deep channel of specialization if they are going to attain any recognition. Consequently, they can become myopic not only to the great philosophical and

*theological foundations underwriting modern science, but to
the logic supplied by other disciplines. If these areas are considered, it alters interpretations and conclusions of the data.*

—Anonymous

*If you understood any world besides your own, you would
understand your own much better.*

—George MacDonald

⸺ ∞ ⸺

"FEW SCIENTISTS ACQUAINTED WITH THE chemistry of biological systems at the molecular level," said chemist and
Nobel Laureate Donald Cram, "can avoid being inspired"
(Cram 1990). Scientific naturalists hold that life is more inspiring as the conception of a cosmic accident, rather than life
as the creation of a complex designer. Biology and the fossil
record are disciplines Darwinists summon to support evolution. Fossils are an *origin* science, where the past is retraced to
better understand pathways towards the present. Fossils are
very speculative since DNA and other sources of information
are usually long gone. *Operation* science characterizes current
biological processes like cellular functions, genetics, breeding, etc. Through a hermeneutic of chance, Darwinists will
use present current processes to speculate back through deep
time the supposed pathways of ancestral descent. Though
operation sciences are more testable, Darwinists emphasize

one or the other of these fields when it seems to support their cause. Whichever discipline is used, conjecture is involved when trying to interpret life from random processes, relegating science as still a worldview and interpretation issue.

Molecular phylogeny studies the relationships among groups of organisms through DNA sequences. Basing their premise on the assumption that the similarity of appearance necessitates ancestral relationship, Darwinists presume that the smaller the difference in the DNA of organisms, the more closely related they are. With this assumption, biologists deduce a "molecular clock" from DNA sequences to estimate the age of an organism based on how identical its proteins are. Then they extrapolate back onto fossils these same rates of change and mutation, to guesstimate how long ago phyla had a common ancestor. Assumptions are laden in this practice, and the common ancestor for some species has such a large range (from one billion years to five hundred thirty million years), that nothing short of confusion typifies the ancestral relationships in the fossil record. The problem is, if we had a last universal common ancestor somewhere and the tree of life is more like a bush, we are no more related to insects than to roundworms! Not only does disorientation result when trying to force the idea of a common ancestor onto the data, but contradictions are raised as several scientists point out:

> In sharks, for example, the gut develops from cells in the roof of the embryonic cavity. In lampreys, the gut develops from cells on the floor of the cavity. And in

frogs, the gut develops from cells from both the roof
and the floor of the embryonic cavity. This discovery—that homologous structures can be produced
by different developmental pathways—contradicts
what we would expect to find if all vertebrates share
a common ancestor (Meyer 2007, 44-45).

The problem of convergence will be addressed in another
lesson. But we mention it here to highlight the fact that different species converging on a function by random pathways
conflicts with the primary Darwinian tenet of shared ancestry. New data in science should continually challenge existing paradigms of thought and expand our knowledge of the
unknown. At the same time, science is about precision and
claiming the best argument for the data as we know it. When
an exact pathway is elusive, it is just too easy to postulate something like random convergence or say, "we have yet to determine a cause" when design is the most accurate conclusion for
the data. Chance based Darwinism is held as consensus mostly
by academics who "worship the intellect like an idol...because
it is to them an unknown god," to use Chesterton's words.

Evolution is consensus among academic elites, even
though a majority of the population is skeptical of Darwinism
as the solution to the secrets of life. Evolutionist Richard
Milton admits that "it is high time that consumerism finds
a voice in the public sector and the academic world" (As
quoted in Martin 2008, 118). Consensus is not needed if
something is true and corresponds to reality. Consensus

can have a political motive where academic power-brokers, compensating for something in the data, decree something as fact. Dr. Michael Crichton draws a distinction between consensus and fact, which certainly applies to evolution:

> Consensus is invoked only in situations where the science is not solid enough... Nobody says the consensus is that the sun is 93 million miles away. [Consensus] is a way to avoid debate by claiming that the matter is already settled. Consensus is the business of politics. Science, on the contrary, requires only one investigator who happens to be right, which means that he or she has results that are verifiable by reference to the real world. In science consensus is irrelevant. What is relevant is reproducible results. The greatest scientists in history are great precisely because they broke with the consensus (Crichton 2003).

Truth is not determined by consensus. Though Darwinism originally challenged the tenets of design in the 1800s, it is now held in consensus by a community of accolade-exchanging researchers for political reasons. But the sinking ship has many leaks and is without evidence for its "airtight arguments." One academic declares, "Making a proclamation that evolution is no longer a theory, but a proven fact is just that—a proclamation. It is not testable science. It does not fit within the definition of the Scientific Method" (Martin 2008, 80). Design, however, has proof on all points of the continuum, from fossils, DNA, genetics, mathematics, logic, and probability. It not only surfaces the stress fractures in Darwinism but refutes the theory. If Charles Darwin knew what we know today, he may not have propounded his theory onto the world, and those committed to his premises retain decreasing intellectual integrity. Few of Darwin's contemporaries accepted his hypothesis and he himself expressed doubts to colleagues about his theory. He said with an authenticity not always found in neo-Darwinists today:

> To the question of why we do not find rich fossiliferous deposits belonging to these assumed earliest periods prior to the Cambrian system, I can give no satisfactory answer...The case at present must remain inexplicable; and may truly be urged as a valid argument against the views here entertained (Darwin 1872, Chap. 10).

MIDPOINT QUESTIONS:

What are the two areas of science Darwinists tap into for support, and when do they use them?

What is molecular phylogeny and what are the problems with it?

What are the dual purposes of science and how does Darwinism violate these?

Why is consensus needed when fact is not established?

It is amazing how scientists will settle for conceivability instead of actuality, using their scientific credentials to make non-scientific statements. For such a precise discipline as molecular biology, it is remarkable how often we hear ambiguous language that few seem to question. Technical journals are loaded with terms like "this probably means that…", "this suggests that…" or "we speculate that…". Michael Graziano, Professor of Neuroscience at Princeton University, made the following statement regarding the mystery of consciousness in the brain, "Early in evolution, *perhaps* hundreds of millions of years ago, brains evolved a specific set of computations to construct that model…And then what? Just as fins evolved into limbs and then into wings, the capacity for awareness *probably* changed and took on new functions over time" (Graziano 2013, emphasis added). *Perhaps* and *probably*? How does he know? Was he there? Fins into limbs and then wings runs into a host of impossibilities, not the least of which is cooption. Statements like this violate the empirical method since they are untestable.

Celebrated primatologist Jane Goodall, who studied chimpanzees in Africa, said "that our aggressive tendencies have *probably* been inherited from some ancient primate some six-million years ago" (Goodall 2009, emphasis added). Probably inherited from some ancient primate? Chimp hostility could also be residual to a curse placed on earth and shared emotions could be a common design, not necessarily a product of ancestral lineage across genus or species lines. Hypothesizing with speculate terms like "probably" and "perhaps" is not necessarily wrong in science. But Darwinists don't allow for any other explanation. They act as if statements from a Graziano or a Goodall are bedrock truth. It's interesting how authoritarianism and atheism go together; in a closed system the case is closed and there are no further arguments.

If science is the pursuit of the exact, it is significant how evolutionists will settle for such ambiguity to justify the assumptions of random origins and modification with descent. One example is the saga of mammals to whales, which reverses evolutionary momentum from water to land, to water again! Evolutionist George Fichter cautions that the "fossil evidence is scarce and the precise and complete picture of certacean [whale, dolphin order] evolution remains a bit of a mystery" (Fichter as quoted in Martin 2008, 71). There are countless speculative diagrams of how one form materialized into another with little credible backing. Concludes evolutionist Patterson: "It is easy enough to make up stories of how one form gave rise to another, and to find reasons why the stages should be favoured by natural selection. But such stories are not part of science, for there is no way to put them to the test" (Patterson 1993).

The pathways Darwinists propose for the origin of life are so general they seem akin to fairy tales and historical novels, where facts are reinterpreted and sprinkled in between large matrixes of verbiage and fanciful drama. Biochemist Franklin Harold acknowledged, "There are presently no detailed Darwinian accounts of the evolution of any biochemical or cellular system, only a variety of wishful speculations" (Harold 2001, 205). Another researcher said that the pathways of descent, which Darwinists present, are like trying to run from California to Japan with only a stop in Hawaii; too much is missing. Or it is like trying to connect the dots of a precise circle with three points. University of Chicago evolutionary microbiologist James Shapiro states:

There are no detailed Darwinian accounts for the evolution of any fundamental biochemical or cellular systems, only a variety of wishful speculations. It is remarkable that Darwinism is accepted as a satisfactory explanation for such a vast subject with so little rigorous examination of how well its basic theses work in illuminating specific instances of biological adaptation or diversity (Shapiro 1996, 65).

Evolutionary biology has not come close to solving the problems of complexity in tightly integrated biological systems. And it is a fabrication to claim material mechanisms will ever solve the problems of life in a reductionistic universe (reductionism is where all of reality is reduced to physical elements). Design theorist William Dembski challenges the evolutionist: "Show us detailed, testable, mechanistic models for the origin of life, the origin of the genetic code, the origin of ubiquitous biomacromolecules and assemblages like the ribosome, and the origin of molecular machines like the bacterial flagellum, and intelligent design will die a quick death" (Dembski 2004).

REVIEW QUESTIONS:

If science is the quest for precision, why is so much speculation implied as fact in science journals?

What do evolutionists even say about alleged evolutionary pathways?

What would happen to intelligent design if Darwinism was vindicated from science?

What should happen to evolution if design is objectively and logically concluded?

If Darwinism is still very tenuous, could it be considered a pseudoscience?

LESSON 4

Challenging the Material Assumption of Darwinism

—⊃⊂⊃⊂—

OBJECTIVES:

account for the beginnings of science and man's fading dependence on theology and the metaphysical realm

describe how Darwin was not the founder of his principles but took natural selection to another level from the trends around him

articulate the design emphasis of Darwin predecessor Edward Blythe

explain what "causal closure" is and how it suffocates science today

Icebreaker:

A reasoning being would lose his reason in attempting to account for the great phenomena of nature, had he not a Supreme Being to refer to.

—George Washington

Up to the age of thirty or beyond it, poetry of many kinds...gave me great pleasure, and even as a schoolboy I took intense delight in Shakespeare...Formerly pictures gave me considerable joy, and music very great delight. But now for many years I cannot endure to read a line of poetry: I have tried to read Shakespeare, and found it so intolerably dull that it nauseated me. I have also almost lost any taste for pictures or music...I retain some taste for fine scenery, but it does not cause me the exquisite delight which it formerly did...My mind seems to have become a kind of machine for grinding general laws out of large collections of facts, but why this should have caused the atrophy of that part of the brain alone, on which the higher tastes depend, I cannot conceive...The loss of these tastes is a loss of happiness, and may possibly be injurious to the intellect, and more probably to the moral character, by enfeebling the emotional part of our nature.

—Autobiography of Charles Darwin

G.K. CHESTERTON WROTE, "IF THE cosmos of the materialist is the real cosmos, it is not much of a cosmos. The thing has shrunk" (Chesterton 2009). When theology was "the queen of the sciences," thought was more expansive. People had a true understanding of the world because the *university* system sought the *unity* of God's presence in the *diverse* branches of knowledge; the more educated one became the closer to a knowledge of God one had. By the advent of the scientific revolution, modern science was still another agency to affirm the varied mysteries of a Creator, via the natural and material world. But the empirical science that once complemented theology soon began to eclipse theology and people became enthralled with the complexities of the newfound material realm. Western thought began to doubt the spiritual realm through a

preoccupation with matter and the study of the unbeknownst folds of the natural world. The resulting vacuum was filled in by other philosophies such as naturalism, atheism, and relativism. The emphasis on science led to an unhealthy dependence on materialism as ultimate reality, where life itself was strained to produce answers to the questions of its own meaning. Through the difficulties in his own life, such as the death of a daughter, Darwin himself became disillusioned with God and became susceptible to atheistic naturalism and the changing tides of science leading up to the 1800s. The erosion of Darwin's faith was subtle by degrees where he, in his own words,

> had gradually come... to see that the Old Testament from its manifestly false history of the world... from its attributing to God the feelings of a revengeful tyrant, was no more to be trusted than the sacred books of the Hindoos, or the beliefs of any barbarian...I gradually came to disbelieve in Christianity as a divine revelation...Thus disbelief crept over me at a very slow rate, but was at last complete. The rate was so slow that I felt no distress, and have never since doubted even for a single second that my conclusion was correct. I can indeed hardly see how anyone ought to wish Christianity to be true (Darwin 1887).

Unfortunately, Darwin was a misguided student of the Word, unregenerate and his knowledge of Scripture uninitiated. (The love of God is a major theme of the Old

Testament and biblical truth is always jettisoned before replaced with a counterfeit). The concept of natural selection was already discovered in nature long before Darwin presented it, traced back to ancient Greek philosophers. But Darwin predecessor Edward Blythe observed localized and individual differences within species through some kind of natural process. Blythe correctly noted it as a way of keeping species within certain boundaries, as a conservative force for sifting out unfit individuals in the environment. The process was not linked to chance as some kind of dynamic generative force. As an advocate of design, he reasoned that because species do not blend and migrate too far, natural selection is a quality-control process to keep nature in check.

Darwin got caught up in the momentous scientific materialism of the day and proposed natural selection as a generating force capable of producing new species. This is quite a leap not only in interpretation of the evidence but also in application, the consequences of which scientists are still trying to vindicate. Perhaps if Blythe had won out, the theory might well be called Blythianism today instead of Darwinism, as an accurate view of what we actually see taking place in nature. Darwin's theory spawned new thought and a host of new positions between creationism and random natural selection, positions such as *theistic evolution* and *process theology*. New questions were launched: "To what extent are natural causes involved in creation?" "What is God's role in nature?" "Does God exist at all?" "Did He get the ball rolling and then let the secondary causes take over, or is He personally active?" "Are secondary causes operating under His complete sovereignty heretical?" "Is God evolving with creation?" If learned men wrestled with some of these questions for centuries, Darwin's book spurred new application to them. The following quote reveals the attrition in Darwin's mind away from God's active involvement in his life.

> I see no good reason why the views given in this volume should shock the religious feelings of any one...A celebrated author and divine has written to me that 'he has gradually learnt to see that it is just as noble a conception of the Deity to believe that He created a few original forms capable of self-development into other and needful forms, as to believe that He required a fresh act of creation to supply the voids caused by the action of His laws' (Darwin 1859).

Because the shift was subtle, from instant creation of many life forms to life as sourced in one living filament, even religious leaders became induced. Darwinism is completely sold on the philosophy that scientific materialism explains and incorporates all of organic life. Although there are some movements to retain God's involvement in science on some level, as far as matter, movement, and energy are concerned, life is a closed system that operates by unbroken natural laws, or what some call "causal closure." Causal closure means that no outside metaphysical or divine influence exists or can get into the system.

Though having flirted with the concept of God in the universe, even physicist Stephen Hawking leans more on a Darwinian view. With how much we do not yet know, it is baffling how he could say, "God may exist, but science can explain the universe without a need for a creator" (Hawking, 2010). That depends on what he means by "explain." Science can answer certain *how* questions but is unequipped in the *why* questions.

MIDPOINT QUESTIONS:

Is it important that a well-developed metaphysical theology (Greek and Christian thought) came before the advent of modern science? Would the age of science have been possible if the order were reversed?

Why does science place so much emphasis on a closed system of unguided natural forces for the origins of life?

Is it possible scientists know God exists, but marginalize Him as irrelevant for other reasons? What happened to Darwin himself?

Someone said, "If you really want to understand a movement, learn how it began." How does this apply to Darwinism?

In Darwinism, life is comprised *of* mechanical systems as much as life is an emergence *from* mechanical processes. But design scientists say that "if nature, as naturalism requires, is a closed nexus of undirected natural causes, then nature knows nothing about the functional nature of those descriptions" (Dembski 2004, 104). Undirected causes cannot produce mind and knowledge, (see Epilogue for the problems of consciousness as a product of elements).

Nature as both the cause as well as the outgrowth of its own process leads to a fallacy of composition. A fallacy of composition says that because a table is made out of wood, the table is wood, or since a house is made of bricks, the house is a brick, or because conversations comprise movements of air molecules, that conversations are nothing more than sounds. However, there is something more in the final product of life that is not reducible to its material components. The concept of synergy, where the whole is greater than the sum of its parts, refutes this fallacy of composition. As humans, we are more than an aggregate of biomacromolecules and as C.S. Lewis concluded, "Ultimately, man cannot be studied, only known." With organisms, mechanisms cannot account for the origin of mechanisms because machines cannot produce what it means to be alive. Machinelike aspects of organisms may be empirically observed, but that does not mean the organism is a machine. As D.H. Lawrence reminds us, "I am not a mechanism, an assembly of various sections" (Lawrence 2012).

Nature does not have what it takes within itself to produce life. We are not arguing that nature does not contribute the raw materials for life in some direct, indirect or facilitating way. The question is whether those raw materials contain within themselves the power and capacity to produce life. Since they do not, *what* has the power and capacity *in conjunction* with nature to produce life? Natural causes never produce things ex nihilo. When they materialize things, they do so by reworking other things. The rifts between the inorganic and organic worlds, as well as the differing layers of complexity, are too great to be determined by natural forces alone.

In the struggle to identify the problems they are trying to resolve, Darwinists argue in a circle. For example, they say that the surviving species are the ones that are the fittest; but, then they say the fittest are those that survive. Harvard professor Ernst Mayr has said that we have no idea what happens in speciation, but then he says evolution is a *fact*. Darwinian mechanisms are assumed in order to be defended, and Darwinists presuppose the things they are trying to establish as their conclusions. Even evolutionary philosopher Thomas Nagel admits, "One doesn't show that something doesn't require explanation by pointing out that it is a condition of one's existence," (Nagel 2011, 95). Fallacies of composition refute a pure mechanistic origin for life and the magical arrangement of materials by undirected processes in a closed system. Only intelligent design supplies the missing piece in a profound intention called information. Darwin himself assumed a closed system and a deterministic view of the cosmos when he said, "everything nature is the result of fixed laws" (Darwin 1887). But he didn't think through this well enough and punted the problem down the field. Where did the laws of physics come from since all laws have lawgivers? Were these laws prior to or "co-contingent" with the universe? How does natural law channel random chance and coevolve with it at the same time? A closed system does not have within it the power and capacity to produce life; there is something more to life that is anterior to life, yet existent with life. Intelligent design supplies the missing piece in a profound intention called information.

Review Questions:

What is a fallacy of composition and how does naturalism lead to the illogic of this fallacy?

In what sense do Darwinists argue in a circle?

How does design refute a closed-nexus explanation for the systems of life?

Darwin's Conspiracy and the Problem of the Mechanisms

⎯ ∞∞∞ ⎯

OBJECTIVES:

state the Darwinian mechanisms and how they differ

describe the major problems in each mechanism for generating new organisms

articulate where design repudiates the two mechanisms

provide examples that validate design and refute Darwinism

Icebreaker:

...between being and not-being, which are the extremes in creation, there can be no medium, and therefore no succession...when the matter is already perfectly disposed for the form, it receives it in an instant...Now in creation nothing is prerequisite on the part of the matter, nor is anything wanting to the agent for action. It follows that creation takes place in an instant.

—Thomas Aquinas

———— ✴ ————

Science writer Robert Sawyer said, "That natural selection can produce changes within a type is disputed by no one, not even the staunchest creationist. But that it can transform one species into another — that, in fact, has never been observed" (Sawyer 2009). For an envisaged transformation of species, Darwinists hold to two fundamental mechanisms, *natural selection* and *random variation.* The mechanisms are problematic, especially when chance is inserted into equation. Darwin himself proposed that chance based natural selection is the restricting dynamic in nature once life somehow originated. Neo-Darwin biologists emphasize the unguided mechanism of random variation and mutation as the laboratory for the generation of new life.

For some science writers, natural selection is confused with variation and implies the origination of materials, where nature is consciously capable of selecting among organisms and *foreseeing* what traits will benefit an organism in the future. Thus, natural selection can wondrously do all of this while making the necessary adjustments in the present to bring these traits about. The problem is, if natural selection is blind and nonteleological (where there is no design or ultimate cause in nature), it is without plan or purpose. With such intricate life forms, the theory is proscribed with powers of planning the theory says it doesn't have. As two design scientists point out, "Animals on ancient earth did not know they were supposed to evolve in such a way that more complex creatures could appear" (Rana and Ross 2015).

Darwinists can lack clarity in the concept. Natural selection is not a creating force in biology nor is it capable of producing new species, as some propose. It is a scaling back, restrictive dynamic. Breeders are often used as examples of what natural selection can do, such as when they produce new show dogs or larger cattle. But the breeders are not creating anything new. They are merely reshuffling existing genes; the presence of a breeder, or in this case nature's breeder, is doing the reshuffling! Design theorists disagree not so much with natural selection in a narrow sense, when certain selective pressures in the environment can bring out varying gene expressions already present in organisms. Everyone accepts the fact that species can adapt and take on a small range of characteristics, depending on their surroundings. But this is adaptation, not macroevolution.

The Darwin family dubbed the term "natural selection" to parallel what breeders do when they select for different traits, calling it "nature's breeder." Darwin theorized and personified that nature itself could produce the differences we see in selective breeding, yet with much more effect if given enough time. Design theorists reply that time, in itself, is no guarantee of change in a closed system. Decades of genetic biology have failed to uncover anything more than changes in species, and nothing above the genus level. Natural selection is only a force for preserving, not transforming species.

MIDPOINT QUESTIONS:

How do Darwinists confuse the abilities in the mechanisms and why is natural selection false as a generating means?

What process did Darwin observe to develop his theory of natural selection?

What does nonteleological mean?

If natural selection is blind and without purpose, what is the forward-looking dynamic in natural selection that can anticipate future functions?

How do design advocates respond to the natural selection engine?

Random variation is the other major mechanism of Darwinism, also known as mutation. In commenting on the generating force behind evolution, the late evolutionary biologist Lynn Margulis was critical of the expanded range Darwinists grant mutation. She said, "New mutations don't create new species; they create offspring that are impaired" (Margulis 2006). We will discover how correct this statement is. If natural selection is the

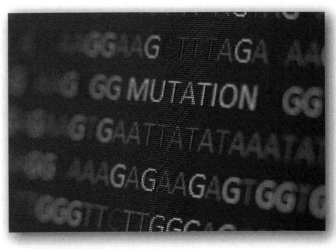

pairing down mechanism in the morphing of species, random variation is the alleged generative force in the Darwinian model. Though Darwinists can sometimes confuse which of the two mechanisms is assigned random variation, mutation is where chance is inserted into the naturalistic framework. Mutation has two basic categories, point mutation and full-length chromosome mutation. In *point mutation*, changes are seen in the individual nucleotide base letters of A, C, T, and G in the DNA molecule. These are small scale random changes of coding in single protein molecules.10

The problem with point mutation is that because the changes are on such a small, individual level, they provide no evidence for macroevolution or anything close to species morphing genome changes. Also, most mutations are harmful or deleterious and result in less than optimal organisms of decreased fitness and survivability. *If natural selection weeds out the less than optimal arrangements and changes are less likely to be passed down, where are the novel life forms?* Mutation as the generator of novel life forms holds two contradictory dynamics that render the premise implausible. Evolution requires the procreation of novel life forms to expand into unique species. However, it is only the dominant populations [that] survive. If information rich hybrids are needed to expand species population sets, the new biodiverse life forms are *not* typically what attract mates! New varieties wouldn't matriculate or be established into principal classifications.

For thousands of years, people have known about breeding and the effects of keeping weaker animals out of the line, even if they couldn't articulate the genetic process. But in these cases, there was an overseer or designer. Darwin, however, put the whole impetus on undirected and random secondary causes. What has actually been observed in organisms is that when the environmental pressure has been reduced, the benefit of a mutation tends to be lost, which is not progress but sideways movement at best. To understand the process on a genetic level, imagine what would happen if some of the words in the Bible are randomly changed. Would the book be improved? Random changes and point mutation decrease the content and likelihood of meaningful information. Darwinists cannot adequately explain why we see optimal creatures continually passed down and reproduced.

The other type of mutation, reputed to be a generative process of Darwinism, is *chromosome mutation*. This is where entire sections of DNA (and not just individual pairs) are repositioned in the gene by chance. But again, this is just rearrangement with no new novel information being created. Natural causes never really create but only surface a limited range of features by reworking other things, as dictated by the law of conservation of

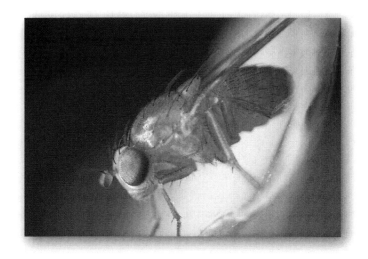

information. In reality, major changes require extensive coordinated adaptations, which in turn require extraordinary amounts of novel functional genetic information. Evolutionary biologists have identified other supposed generative mechanisms such as gene transfer, symbiogenesis, genetic drift, and self-organizational properties. But these are still subject to the same problems the two mechanisms of evolutionary theory suffer from.

A profitable area of study in testing the generative abilities of these mechanisms is the fruit fly (drosophila). The fruit fly has quick reproductive cycles, a short life span and a genome that is easily manipulated. When artificial pressures are created to mimic mutations, some biologists point to the new novel features in drosophila as evidence of evolution. To be sure, "new" features have resulted, and evolutionary bloggers laud these as examples of evolution in action. But the attributes that result are monstrosities such as additional legs or four wings instead of two, with no new structures generated. The products are deleterious with little functional and survival value to the insects. The bottom line is that natural selection is not an adequate causal power. *Natural selection cannot select for future functions that are not already present in helping organisms survive or reproduce* (Dembski 2004, 159). And mutation is not a generative dynamic because organisms are never better, just different and usually worse. Making the transition from an old to a new function is not a task for which any Darwinian mechanism is equipped for, and we cannot logically conceive of life-forms moving up the phylogenetic tree.

Mutation theoretically floods the gene pool with new information, new codes and novel proteins. But a serious question arises. How can a species maintain its current biological functions for survival, while experimenting and freelancing with mutation? Darwinists believe they have found the answer in gene duplication. Genes do make copies of themselves, for cell division and the overall growth of an organism. Darwinists hold that both the coding and non-coding sections of the genome endure what is known as *neutral evolution*, where prolonged changes in the nucleotide sequences allegedly do not interrupt the functions of the organism. With enough time, an ensuing new gene sequence can be naturally selected to produce a new protein. This notion seems to allow the duplicate gene to experiment and freelance, while the original gene can do its job and code for functions in the cell. Sounds possible in theory, but when the details are probed Darwinism is again thrust back into fairy tale status.

Genomes can vary throughout many generations when the so-called mutations seek out new base sequences. But there are problems with duplicate genes fashioning a transmutation of species where reptiles ultimately generate mammals, for example, or where fish produce amphibians. How does the replicate gene evolve into an entirely new gene? How does the facsimile gene obtain a totally new function? It violates the problems surfaced with cooption. Darwinists *never* give any details or step by step sequences of events. Also, any new information produced in the copy gene is really a variant of the original gene. It is not a totally new gene and any increase through duplication is trivial. Gene duplication does not provide a meaningful increase in specified and complex information required for new proteins and functions. And most obvious of all is that mutation doesn't explain where the complex forms came from to begin with! (Luskin 2007).

The only area of evolution gene duplication supports is microevolution or adaptation, where alleles (variant forms

of a given gene) will occasionally lead to different pheno-
types (changes in physical appearance) as brought out by
certain selective pressures. Scientists can accuse those who
believe in design (or even creation) as committing intellectual suicide. But when pressed for step by step details
in how new genes arise, the intellectual bankruptcy is on
the Darwinian side when they gloss over the details, hide
behind ambiguous general scenarios, and rely on blind
chance. At this point, some biologists can get thin skinned
when they lose the substance argument and have resorted
to name calling, labeling design theorists as petty for not
just accepting the whole conjecture (Luskin 2007). But the
clearest thinkers in any discipline are those who operate
from the correct metaphysical base.

Intelligent design says that because biological systems show amazing complexity, the life of the system
is not exclusively reducible to its mechanisms. It comes
down to information, which is intelligent design's major contribution in reworking the theory of origins.
The only way to flood new genetic information into the
gene pool is by altering the nucleotide bases of the individual genes, *not* by mutations that alter simple protein
molecules. Point and chromosome mutation do not add
new genetic information into the gene consortium; they
tweak but they do not create. And gene duplication only
supports adaptation. We might say to a Darwinist, that if

information precedes material activity, what is the vision or forward-looking dynamic for evolutionary progress according to a reductionistic framework? If biological systems are only utilized for the moment, where does the plan come from for future upgrades? How does the generative mechanism overcome the deleterious nature of mutation and the destructive tendencies of the second law of thermodynamics? And what is the dynamic that continually overcomes *phylogenetic inertia*, which is a tendency in organisms to maintain an average morphology and limited variability around a population average? Even biology supports the premise that the physical is subject to the metaphysical.

REVIEW QUESTIONS:

What are the two types of mutation and what are their real effects that Darwinists don't like to emphasize?

What are the problems with gene duplication as the *engine room* for mutation and macroevolutionary change?

How does design repudiate the Darwin mechanism of mutation?

What creature in lab tests confounds Darwinism and why?

What is *phylogenetic inertia* and how does it work against the Darwinian hypothesis?

What questions could we pose to Darwinists about the two mechanisms?

Irreducible Complexity and Fully Formed Life Systems

—∞∞∞—

OBJECTIVES:

explain why intelligent design is its own theory and not a default position when evolution is debunked

articulate irreducible complexity and give illustrations for it

ICEBREAKER:

I believe that pure thinking will do more to educate a man than any other activity he can engage in...to let one idea beget another, and that another, till the mind teems with them...to join thought with thought like an architect till a whole edifice has been created within the mind...to bound upward through illimitable space and downward into the nucleus of an atom; and all this without so much as moving from our chair or opening the eyes—this is to soar above all the lower creation and come near to the angels of God.

—A. W. Tozer

———❧———

CHARLES DARWIN ONCE SAID, "To kill an error is as good a service as, and sometimes even better than, the establishing of a new truth or fact." The "error" Darwinists deem to correct iss any scientific dependence on the Bible and its "unadorned" accounts of creation, natural theology, and history. However, is natural selection under fixed laws in a closed system an established fact? There are only two options for the origin of life and killing the errors in Darwinian assumptions may be a service to science. The two types of evolution that design advocates in general, and creationists in particular, strongly disagree with are macroevolution and chemical evolution. The next several lessons will chop down the tall tale of macroevolution, while chemical evolution will be dealt with later in the study.

Macroevolution is mandatory for the Darwinian model to be proven; it is where the major changes in the animal kingdom are theorized to have occurred. Macroevolution is also where the descent of all organisms can allegedly be traced back to a universal common ancestor. Darwinian evolutionists support their theory from the disciplines of *biology* and *paleontology* (the fossil record) and do so with varying degrees of emphases when it is convenient for their cause. Generally, the fossil evidence is more limited since the past is gone, and there is usually no DNA left over for analysis. Thus, current biology can be the focus and great frontier for material evolutionists. When answers lead to more questions, Darwinists often hide behind the great unknown of cyberspace in cells and say, in so many words, "we don't know yet. The answer is probably there, we just don't know yet." But science requires the most plausible explanation for the data at any given moment. Design adopts a wide array of information into its theory, with greater harmony and less deformity of the data.

There are only two competing theories for the origin of life, accident or design. Oxford biologist Richard Dawkins admitted that, "Superficially, the obvious alternative to chance is an intelligent Designer" (Dawkins 1982, 130). Like shoveling out water from a bucket, the empty space created by Darwinism is immediately replaced by the evidence for design. The proof for intelligent design is not negative, where a strike against Darwinism makes design look better by default. Rather, the weight of evidence for preexisting design leaves no room for Darwinian chance, which more and more would become a fable of education. With eloquence and a bit of irony,

Darwin himself said, "Great is the power of steady mis-representation." Darwinism has been faithfully purveyed by neo-Darwinists, who infuse chance based natural selection in their interpretations. However, as science unveils the layered complexity in nature, it is Darwinism that has steadfastly misrepresented science as design becomes more undeniable on all fronts and branches of biology.

MIDPOINT QUESTIONS:

What are the two bodies of evidence Darwinists draw from when trying to prove macroevolution?

What is a common response Darwinists give when design is the most plausible explanation of the data?

How are evolution and design interpretations linked?

Despite the rhetorical sleight of hand and wordplay Darwinian scientists employ when interpreting the data, biology has not legitimately verified Darwin's assumptions since the mid-1800s. In fact, Darwin himself had more honesty than many biologists today when he wrote prophetically, "Why, if species have descended from other species by insensibly fine gradations, do we not everywhere see innumerable transitional forms?" (Darwin 1859, Chapter 6). Even today "innumerable transitional forms" have not been corroborated. Biological systems have layers of hierarchy and dimensional aspects in the material components of their complex structures that defy undirected chance.

A pillar of design that biologists have observed in biological systems is irreducible complexity, which compounds the evolutionary problem. Irreducible complexity means that molecular machines are complex and integral in the life of the cell. That is, they do not develop incrementally or by stealing functions from other systems to produce a new system. The machines just appear, with as much complexity as needed to function and each part requisite to the operation of the whole system. Molecular biologist Michael Behe, who coined the term, defines irreducible complexity as such:

> a single system composed of several well-matched, interacting parts that contribute to the basic function, wherein the removal of any one of the parts causes the system to effectively cease functioning. An irreducibly complex system cannot be produced directly (that is, by continuously improving the initial function, which continues to work by the same mechanism) by slight, successive modifications of a precursor system, because

any precursor to an irreducibly complex system that is missing a part is, by definition, nonfunctional. An irreducibly complex biological system, if there is such a thing, would be a powerful challenge to Darwinian evolution (Behe 1996, 39).

Behe says that further simplifying a biological system, or coopting parts out of the system into another, would destroy the whole molecular function. There are more and more biologists affirming the arguments for irreducible complexity as a step away from Darwinism since Michael Behe's landmark book was published. They are not theists necessarily, but the objective realities in science are moving them in that direction.

There is no evidence that organisms develop slowly through indirect pathways or were modified with descent in some progressive and increasingly complex fashion. Boom, they just appear with integrated and tightly fitting functions, and without slight modifications or associations of descent. Walt Brown, PhD in mechanical engineering from MIT adds, "No component of these complex systems could have evolved without placing the organism at a selective disadvantage until the component's evolution was complete. All evidence points to intelligent design" (Brown 2008, 19).

One way to illustrate irreducible complexity is with a mousetrap. All the parts of a mouse trap must be pertinent and present for the system to work, and each part is formed for that system. Take one part away and the mousetrap cannot function. The same is true for biological systems, as all parts just appear without any pathways of progression. The major components of the eye, for example, must all be present to function. The Darwinian mechanism of natural selection is an *instant gratification feature* where current functionality of each system is necessary for the theory. From a utilitarian perspective, which is endemic to Darwinian philosophy, what is the use of half an eye? What was the function of the parts of the eye in the gradual evolution of the eye, before the eye was formed or any use discerned? No convincing pathways of any detail are given. Interestingly,

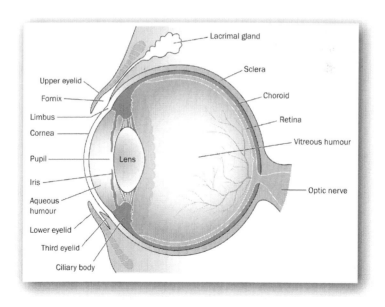

Darwin himself commented on the precision of the eye with a statement that is as true today as when he wrote it,

> To suppose that the eye, with all its inimitable contrivances for adjusting the focus to different distances, for admitting different amounts of light, and for the correction of spherical and chromatic aberration, could have been formed by natural selection, seems, I freely confess, absurd in the highest possible degree (Darwin 1971, 167).

Whether it is the smallest of biological systems or the largest of creatures, the same principle applies. If we extrapolate the myriads of irreducibly complex molecular systems within the cell onto full-fledged organisms, we get what are known as *complete adaptation packages.* That is, animals just appear and ready to go. The giraffe is an interesting example on a large-scale species level. Darwin thought the long neck adapted to the utility of eating leaves that are positioned high on trees, which even a child might reason to. However, a problem arises in how to get blood to the giraffe's head. A strong heart is now needed, which the giraffe happens to have. But then how does the giraffe drink? When it bends down, the blood vessels in the neck and head would burst. According to evolutionary theory, the giraffe would need a new, compensating function to prevent death; however, it wouldn't know it needs it until it has died.

And dead things don't evolve anything. A graduated, modified with descent animal would have never arrived because one function that enables survival is thwarted by another that causes extinction. Fortunately, the giraffe is preequipped all at once with a strong heart to get blood to the head, as well as pressure sensors in the arteries of the neck to signal for the giraffe to stop drinking (Dembski and Wells 2008, 40). The giraffe is designed with all the arrangements necessary for its environment.

As in the mousetrap example above, all of these systems in the giraffe appear together. They had to be co-created or occur all at once in a complete adaptation package, not accrued by adoptive cumulative changes over time. This is a major problem for the Darwinist, as two design theorists point out: "A functionally integrated system consists of parts that are tightly adapted to one another and thus make the system's function sensitive to isolated changes of these parts. Remove one part of the core and you can't recover the system's basic function" (Dembski and Wells 2008, 146). The giraffe is but one example of the many fully formed complete adaptation packages in nature. Instead of bottom up evolution assumed by modification with descent, the giraffe and other organisms appear to have a *top-down design* when the package deals of irreducible complexity are considered. The structures are so interdependent that a top-down design is the only option capable of "anticipating the total engineering requirements of organisms like the giraffe" (Dembski and Wells 2008, 42).

REVIEW QUESTIONS:

What is irreducible complexity and how does it deal a major blow to Darwinism?

What evidence contradicts the Darwinian philosophy of a utilitarian, "present function" for each part in a biological system?

Define a "complete adaptation package" and give an illustration of it.

Why are organisms better explained by "top down" design rather than "bottom up" evolutionary origin?

The Poster Child for Irreducible Complexity

— ∞∞∞ —

OBJECTIVES:

show how the bacterial flagellum supports irreducible complexity

explain how molecular and manmade machines reflect the law of design

illustrate the fatal errors of cooption as a reply to irreducible complexity

ICEBREAKER:

The scientific way of looking at the world is not wrong any more than the glassmaker's way of

looking at the window. This way of looking at things has its very important uses. Nevertheless, the window was placed there not to be looked at, but to be looked through; the world has failed in its purpose unless it too is looked through and the eye rests not on it, but on its God.

—B. B. Warfield

DARWINIAN IDOLATRY FOCUSES ON THE physical world only and tries to explain the existence of life from matter alone. Yet Darwin, himself, said his theory would absolutely break down if "numerous, successive, slight modifications" in any complex organ could not be demonstrated. Irreducible complexity demonstrates how the slightest of modifications in the cell are impossible by random mechanisms and Darwinian assumptions. A premier biomolecular example for irreducible complexity is the bacterial flagellum system, which is a poster child for the intelligent design movement. The bacterial flagellum is an irreducibly complex protein machine with a whiplike tail that propels bacteria through its watery environment. It is basically a rotary motor with the same characteristics of motors that human engineers design, all with a propeller, rotor, stator, driveshaft, hook joint, bushings, O-rings, and mounting disks.

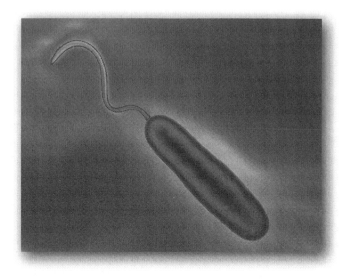

The tail of the bacterial flagellum rotates bidirectionally at extremely fast speeds and, according to Harvard biophysicist Howard Berg, is the "most efficient machine in the universe" (Berg 2016). The tail averages twenty thousand rpms but can reach up to one hundred thousand rpms while still being able to change directions in a quarter of a turn! The flagellum is necessary for the bacteria to get food and requires twenty-five proteins in the correct sequence to form. Yet the absence of any one of these core parts would result in a complete loss of motor function (Dembski and Wells 2008, 149). Simultaneous construction is absolutely mandatory for survival. To underscore Aquinas, "in creation nothing is prerequisite on the part of the matter... creation takes place in an instant."

The most amazing thing about molecular machines like the bacterial flagellum is how similar they are to our man-made ones. Preexisting designs in nature have nothing to do with man's influence, yet they precede human designs with similar functions according to the laws of nature as we know them. When the motor was invented, the blueprints of natural systems such as the bacterial flagellum were unknown. Inventors could not copy the natural design because it was so small (eight million of the bacterial motors could fit inside the circular cross section of a human hair!) and the electron microscope was not yet invented. After the microscope was invented, it was discovered that the natural design preexisted our human fabrications from the beginning, with great consistency of pattern. This is no coincidence since the law of design that characterizes the universe is everywhere; natural and human motors are both intended. MIT engineer Walt Brown writes:

Most complex phenomena known to science are found in living systems--including those involving electrical, acoustical, mechanical, chemical, and optical phenomena. Detailed studies of various animals also have revealed certain physical equipment and capabilities that the world's best designers, using the most sophisticated technologies, cannot duplicate (Brown 2008, 19).

Midpoint Questions:

What is the bacterial flagellum and what are its core parts?

How does the bacterial flagellum support the law of design?

What is amazing about the bacterial flagellum as it relates to man-made motors?

Of course, Darwinists are not without reply to this "problem" of irreducible complexity. Ingeniously, they have crafted a term called "cooption" to justify gradual Darwinian pathways of descent. Cooption is conceived where parts from previously targeted systems break free and are

"coopted" into a new novel system. In other words, parts drift off from one system and then are borrowed and utilized for a new system through an unsuspended and ambiguous period of time. This concept is the engine room that attempts to make mutation a reality. But there are numerous problems with this fabrication of the evidence. First, how could a thing evolve from one function and be totally coordinated for another function? Cooption stacks coincidence on coincidence, like randomly picking out parts at Radio Shack and hoping to have the right components to make a computer. Or it would be like taking a bolt from a car, a washer from an airplane, a nut from a refrigerator and randomly hoping they would a fit a carburetor for a lawnmower. What we actually see with extremely precise and complex biological systems is that each part is specifically tailored for its own system, without trials and restarts.

You cannot add a component to one system and then make it indispensable to the original system. *In other words, it is impossible to coopt for parts and graft them into a structure whose very function is coevolving with the structure.* There is no forward-looking dynamic to know where to find a part if the structure itself is codeveloping without a preexisting plan or destination. In the trial-and-error process, there would be interfering cross-reactions with other proteins. As Dembski and Wells clarify, "Finding a subsystem of a functional system that performs some other function does not show that the subsystem evolved into the system" (Dembski and Wells 2008, 154).

Design engineers constantly use basic design plans that carry over from one system to another under the laws of physics as we know them. No less is true in biology. "The need to function within a common universe puts common physical and chemical requirements on all organisms" (Davis and Kenyon 1989, 35). For unguided, chance-based Darwinian mechanisms, there is no forward-looking dynamic for all the parts of a bacterial flagellum working in another system to spontaneously break free and form new, tightly coordinated systems. Biological parts are tailored to the specifics of the system, which cooption cannot specify. Precise and tightly coordinated biological systems, consistently fashioned from information, are clearly designed.

A bird provides a large-scale species-level example of the cooption problem. All of a bird's organs are designed and contribute to the one action called flight. It has hollow bones, feathers, the absence of a bladder, and a mother who does not carry her young, all contributing to lighter weight. From a functional perspective, a bird is a fully formed, final-end, complete adaptation package. What its independent parts were used for, grafted from, or morphed into is unknown. To say it evolved is pure science fiction and if imagination has its place in science, this is not it. As evolutionary biologist Pierre Paul Grasse warned, "There is no law against day dreaming, but science must not indulge in it" (Grasse 1977, 103). Science is about the best explanation of the evidence, yet Darwinists only provide abstract scenarios without tenable or detailed evolutionary pathways, either direct or indirect. We can firmly say that "cooption is not an option" to explain irreducible complexity in nature.

To be sure, Darwinists are not without reply to the premise of irreducible complexity and the problems of cooption. Brown University molecular biologist Kenneth Miller cites a 1998 study by Musser and Chan, who outline the evolutionary tree of the cytochrome c oxidase protein pump with "impressive detail." Cytochrome c oxidase is a membrane protein in the cell which acts as an enzyme and causes a chemical reaction in the making of food. Since oxygen is unstable and reactive, the energy from the reaction acts as a molecular pump to power ions across the membrane. Two of the six proteins in the proton pump are comparable to a bacteria enzyme known as the cytochrome bo3 complex, and some scientists theorize that the smaller working assemblies adapted to fit newer, novel functions. Miller is one of those scientists who asks and answers his own question, "Could this mean that *part* of the proton pump evolved from a working cytochrome bo3 complex? Certainly." He calls similarity of individual parts in biological systems "selectable functions," attempting to justify co-option and rendering the hypothesis of irreducible complexity "falsified."

Similar appearances in biological systems necessitating close relations or linkage by descent is tantamount to syntactical gymnastics. The resemblance of function, the use of similar molecules and the likeness of materials does not guarantee cooption. These similarities could easily mean common design when juxtaposed with current laws of physics. Miller's interpretation of the data on a micro level is similar to the misstep Darwin made in morphology, where similarity of appearance in structures means ancestral relationship. It all goes back to one's philosophy of science, what one sees and wants to see. In his attempt to refute the irreducible complexity of the bacterial flagellum, Miller admits that he himself has "not provided a detailed, step-by-step explanation of the evolution of the flagellum," and then says that detailed pathways in proving the descent of molecular systems are "not required"! (Miller 2003). No direct pathway is given.

REVIEW QUESTIONS:

What is cooption and how is it untenable as a concept?

Even if parts are borrowed from other systems, how does this point to a designer?

What is an example of a large-scale, irreducibly complex total adaptation package?

What is the weakness in molecular biologist Kenneth Miller's argument for co-option and his attack on intelligent design?

Is it necessarily true that similarity of appearance or function means ancestral relationship?

The Origin of the Species or the Spurious?

———◦∞∞◦———

OBJECTIVES:

distinguish what speciation is and what it is not

state the crucial role speciation plays in Darwin's theory

refute the classic example of speciation known as Darwin's finches

describe clearly what takes place in adaptation

disprove the argument of incipient speciation with the example of bacteria

Icebreaker:

Man is the result of a purposeless and natural process that did not have him in mind.

—George Gaylord Simpson

If evolution destroys anything, it does not destroy religion but rationalism...If evolution simply means that a positive thing called an ape turned very slowly into a positive thing called a man...[then there is] no such thing as a man for him to change into. It means that there is no such thing as a thing. At best, there is only one thing, and that is a flux of everything and anything. This is an attack not upon the faith, but upon the mind; you cannot think if there are no things to think about. You cannot think if you are not separate from the subject of thought.

—G.K. Chesterton

⸺⸺

Physicist Paul Davies confessed that "Many investigators feel uneasy stating in public that the origin of life is a mystery, even though behind closed doors they admit they are baffled" (Davies 1999, 26). This is no more true than in the subject of speciation, a focal point of evolutionary biology. Publicly, proponents of evolution market the theory as established fact; privately, Darwinists still hope that if scientists could observe species changing and undergoing upgrades, then they would vindicate macroevolution. "Speciation," whatever that really means, is crucial for the Darwinist to extrapolate over time the gradation of higher organisms in the taxonomic chart through the modification with descent. But Darwinists can't really articulate the difference between a species, a variation and a transition. *The subject is unnecessarily complicated by a rapacious commitment to the assumption that similarity of appearance necessarily means ancestral relationship.* This Darwinian assumption has led to confusion as to what a species is. With over two dozen definitions, there is no agreement among biologists in classifying a species. Because they believe it better helps their cause, many Darwinists have settled on Ernst Mayr's biological species concept, which defines species as "groups of interbreeding natural populations that are reproductively isolated from other groups" (Mayr 1942, 120). While this definition seems to vindicate Darwinists' definition of speciation, it actually lowers the bar because it says little about how isolated interbreeding populations came to be; it only describes how isolated species are interbreeding now. If there is neither speciation nor a larger morphing of classifications on the taxonomic chart, Darwinism is dead.

An irony of Darwin's 1859 book, *The Origin of the Species*, is that he speaks little about *origins* of species, but only modifications once they somehow appeared. Where he does hint at origins, he retains language commensurate with the creation account of Genesis. Towards the end of *Origin*, he writes: "Life, with its several powers, *having been originally breathed* into a few forms or into one…are being evolved." Interestingly, it seems like Darwin borrowed the same language; when God formed man from the dust, Genesis 2:7 says "He breathed into his nostrils the breath of life." And Genesis 1:30 says everything has "the breath of life." Though it has been over 150 years since Darwin's time, all we have observed since then are localized adaptations, not speciation. In fact, there has been no clear case of speciation or a verified missing link. Darwin himself, who formed much of his theory from the fossil record, had many doubts that evolutionists don't tell us. Darwin's misgivings have been affirmed in the many years since his book. He wrote, "Why is not every geological formation and every stratum full of such intermediate links? Geology assuredly does not reveal any such finely graduated organic chain… [which] is the most obvious and gravest objection which can be urged against my theory" (Darwin 1964, 189).

To support speciation, Darwin's finches from the Galápagos Islands are an icon of evolution still used to this day. But it does not take much observation to realize that this icon actually backfires as support for the Darwinian premise. Though still in textbooks, the Galápagos finches really display adaptation. Darwin observed that the finches with the larger beaks survived in times of drought, where the finches with smaller beaks died off. The larger-beaked finches could crack open the shells of their food supply, but the smaller-beaked finches could not, and they subsequently starved to death. It appeared as though random selection and environmental pressure were a generative force, as larger beaked finches morphed and created something new. What really happened was small-scale selection, adaptation, and gene reshuffling—not speciation and novel structures. It has since been shown that the smaller-beaked finches returned on the islands after the drought subsided! A trophy of Darwinism for decades is really a case of adaptation.

Midpoint Questions:

How is speciation crucial for the Darwinian theory?

What definition of species is held today and why is this unconvincing?

What did Darwin himself admit and what have we really observed in the 150 years since?

What icon of evolution collapses when it is probed, and what is the real story of Darwin's finches on the Galápagos Islands?

Darwin speculated that given enough time, the innocuous adaptations he observed in organisms would migrate into larger changes down the classification chart, resulting in new species. But this Darwinian assumption still has not been observed, no matter how speciation is defined or categorized. One kind of speciation is *allopatric speciation* where species become geographically separated by forces of nature (such as a waterway or a mountain range) and then breed within. Another is *sympatric speciation*, where populations are isolated and nonreproducible within the same geography. With dynamics such as "genetic drift," neo-Darwinists feel they have another mechanism through the tendency of genes to drift away into smaller populations to underwrite the macroevolutionary machine of speciation.

While these elements of speciation are more specifically identified by modern science, they are still different applications of adaptation. And they are answered by the same arguments that devastated the icon of Darwin's finches in the Galápagos, where there was just a *reshuffling in the emphasis or expression of the genes that already existed*. There is no new or novel information generated in any speciation but merely an adaptation of genes, which is sometimes called *secondary speciation*. What we need is evidence for *primary speciation* in the morphing of one species into another to validate the Darwinian assertions. In fact, with adaptation, the reverse usually takes place over time, where there eventually results a *net loss* of genetic information over time. A scaling back of information is the opposite effect necessary for the generation of new novel species under random variation. Also, if novel life forms require varied selective pressures, the great changes in species up the tree of life are beyond the limited range of changes the environment can produce by chance. In other words, the fairly stable range of environmental characteristics needed to produce various life forms is below the standard by which a fantastic morphing of species requires. Darwinian logic falters in its own context.

Darwinists are not without rebuttal to these heavy blows against their theory. They say we have not had "enough time" to study these processes, since these changes take place over millions of years. They also hold that the species we see today are what they call "incipient species," which are "snapshots in time" of animals in the process of change. If played out over a long period or millions of years, they would exhibit larger changes. However, the incipient species argument is answered from tests on bacteria. Bacteria are a preferred organism of study because they can generate in twenty minutes, achieve populations in eighteen hours, and literally hundreds of thousands of generations have been studied for 150 years. The results? No new speciation! (Dembski and Wells 2008). Darwinists may point out that bacterial resistance to new antibiotics is proof of speciation. Evolutionist Colin Patterson wrote, "The development of antibiotic-resistant strains of bacteria, and also of insects resistant to DDT and a host of other recently discovered insecticides, are genuine evolutionary changes" (Patterson 1978). But the obvious problem with this statement is that they are still bacteria! No new organisms are produced, and nothing is moved up the taxonomic chart. This is merely adaptation, a reshuffling of existing matter, and not speciation or anything close to macroevolution. There is no known material mechanism capable of causing genetic modification from which new information can come.

Review Questions:

What definition of speciation do many Darwinists use today, and why is it crucial for macroevolution?

What is adaptation and why is it important to distinguish primary from secondary speciation?

If significant adaptations occur, what really happens to genetic information?

How do bacteria assist the design argument and how would you refute the Darwinian reply?

How would you negate Darwinists who say we are "incipient species"?

There's More to Life Than Genes

———⚭⚭⚭———

OBJECTIVES:

define convergent and divergent evolution

articulate how the convergence of similar structures in unrelated species by chance is improbable

present how the giant and red panda do not display convergence

explain how common design better accounts for similarities in species rather than common descent

specify how genes are not quite the central component in sustaining life, or differentiating among organisms, as once thought

ICEBREAKER:

A little girl asked her mother, "Where do humans come from?"

Her mother answered, "About six million years ago the first human ancestors split off from apes and we have been evolving ever since." Seemingly satisfied, she walked away.

Two days later, the girl asks her father, "Where do humans come from?"

Her father replied, "A long time ago in the Garden of Eden, in what is now Iraq, God made Adam and Eve and humankind came from them."

The girl thought for a moment and said to her father, "Why does Mom say we came from apes, and you say we came from Adam and Eve? Who is right?"

"Well dear, it's very simple," her father answered. "I told you my side of the family, and your mother told you hers."

"PUT SIMPLY," CAMBRIDGE PALEOBIOLOGIST SIMON Conway-Morris stated, "convergence shows that in a real world not all things are possible" (Morris 2003). Convergence is a hallmark feature of evolutionary thought that is brought out to defend Darwin's theory. Convergence is defined as the independent acquisition or evolution of the same biological trait in unrelated organisms. In other words, convergence is where life systems from separate places just happen to descend on very similar or nearly identical forms, by independent pathways and random processes. When homologous animals and those with similar structures are said to have a common origin but later separate, they exhibit a process called *divergent evolution* from which results the famous tree of life. But when animals display similarities from independent lineages, they are assumed to have converged or be *analogous*. That is, through random variation they are reputed to have different descent paths but converge and share remarkable similarities in structure by chance. Though apparently identified in nature, both divergent and convergent evolution are speculations without evidence. Convergence is a magical attempt to explain the similarity of organisms when there is little possibility of divergent ancestral relationship overcoming geographical odds and classification differences. In convergence, we are to believe organisms evolved twice from scratch (by chance) in nearly the same fashion, raising the improbabilities exponentially.

One example presented as convergence is the giant panda and the red panda, both of which inhabit the same bamboo forests in south China. Though biologists have gone back and forth in classifying the two species as separate or similar, the prevailing theory today is that they are from different families. The giant panda is in the bear family, and the red panda is in the raccoon family. Yet they both share an impressive list of features, including the "panda thumb," or radial sesamoid for peeling bamboo bark (though it is not actually a thumb but a protruding bone). If the separate classifications are true, then to explain this coincidence of nature the two species happened to have "converged" on the same blueprint and features by random mutation. In other words, they did not receive their traits by common descent, but the "thumb" coincidently evolved twice from scratch. Another example of convergence in fully developed life-forms pertains to birds, mammals, insects, and fish, which can all fly. We are lead to believe that these unrelated creatures converged on the same function of flight,

all by chance, four times over! (Dembski and Wells 2008, 123).

Chance is at the root of biochemical evolution and, according to Merriam-Webster, is "the assumed impersonal purposeless determiner of unaccountable happenings" (Webster 2016). Evolutionary pathways require a historical sequence of purposeless genetic changes operated on by natural selection. But a serious issue arises. If evolutionary processes are random, scientists should observe no cases where evolution has repeated itself, nor should biochemical designs recur in nature. Chance-based evolutionary processes are unable to retrace the same path, making repeated biological chemical designs in nature exceedingly unlikely. In addition, if things evolved again, they would be totally different given the random nature of the universe. Steven Jay Gould posited that if it were possible to repeat evolutionary events, the outcome would be dramatically different every time. Yet convergence says separate evolutionary paths give rise to the same features by accident, the very thing chance cannot do. It is astonishing to claim that undirected processes and random variation somehow landed on one unique organism. But to claim identical features evolved in separate organisms over and again through random variation in the wild is beyond credulity. Convergence and chance are contradictory features in the same theory.

If life, however, is the product of a designer, then the same designs could repeatedly appear in biochemical systems, which is what we observe. It seems more accurate to accept common design in animals with similar structural blueprints, not only because design is logically coherent, but also because the a priori data corresponds to observed reality. Repeated occurrences in biochemical systems logically point to design. Common features do not necessarily mean common descent nor common convergence, but they could be commonly designed, the most plausible option left out of many science textbooks. Design is a law of reality that typifies existence, and designers often piggyback and cross utilize common ideas without using ancestral parts. If we look at the "evolution" of the Corvette automobile, for example, we see borrowed ideas and similarities over the years. The Corvette changes but it is still a Corvette. It does not "evolve," per se, because it does not have shared or coopted parts. And it still has a designer! (Dembski and Wells 2008).

MIDPOINT QUESTIONS:

What is the difference between convergent and divergent evolution?

How do the giant and the red pandas allegedly support convergence?

Why is random variation a problem as it relates to convergence?

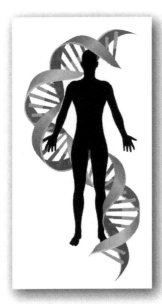

Darwin first argued for shared evolutionary ancestry based on the appearance of shared structures. Convergence is postulated to uphold evolution when different species from separate lineages have similar structures. Fortunately, biology today allows for more objectivity to determine the feasibility of common descent in the area of genetics and DNA. Has genetics carried the Darwinian ball further down the field, or does that also point to design? Because of our materialistic culture, genes get all the attention as the keys to life, and the impression is we are nothing more than the quality of our DNA. But how important are genes, where do they come from, and are they the secrets to life? That we are "nothing more than our genes" is another a fallacy of composition based on scientific propaganda and reductionistic assumptions. There is something more in the final products of life forms than just the assembly of parts.

When molecular biologists supplanted an embryo with the DNA of a different organism, they found that the embryo continued to develop into the original species of the animal for a period of time! They eventually died for other reasons, but what kept them developing according their original blueprints? Genes alone do not control development, as embryos somehow develop without the original genes. The same argument applies to death; the genes in a corpse five minutes after death are the same ones in a living organism. The biblical account is that both man and animals have the "breath of life" (Gen. 2:7, 1:30) and, as far as humans are concerned, "the body without the spirit is dead" (Jas. 2:26). Evolutionary biologist Lynn Margulis confessed, "For all the accomplishments of molecular biology, we still can't tell a live cat from a dead cat." There is more to life than our genes.

Genetics links are mandatory for a singularity of origin from one living filament postulation. Since Mary-Claire Kings' famous study of 1973, chimps are a lauded example of shared genetic content to argue for a common ancestor with humans. We share a 98 percent (95 percent in some studies) similar genetic composition with chimps. While

this sounds impressive, such genetic similarity should make humans virtually identical with chimps. But this begs the following questions. Why are we so different? If chimps and humans are 98 percent genetically similar, why don't we see a replicate species and not just the same genus? If the assumption that biological structures are solely determined by genes, why aren't we more similar to chimps? Looked at from a different angle, if the varying structures between chimps and humans are sourced in different genes, why don't we have more genetic diversity than chimps? Similar genes should not produce such different animals if replicate genes alone control development. We should be more similar.

The problem with the chimp/human comparison is method. A qualitative, direct gene to gene comparison of humans to chimps stacks the deck in favor of the Darwinist argument. Amino acids and proteins are the building blocks for life and the workhorses of the cell. But 95 percent of the human genome is *noncoding* for proteins, so a direct comparison of human and chimp genomes is not particularly relevant. Furthermore, there are more differences between human and chimp DNA than we hear about when whole genomes, and not just genes, are compared. Scientists at the Max Planck Institute compared ten thousand *regions* (not individual genes) and found only two-thirds aligned between the two species. The similarity between humans and chimps drops to 86 percent when insertions and deletions (introns and exons) are considered in the genome. The absence or alteration of even one gene makes a huge difference in formation. Furthermore, parts of the gorilla genome align better with humans than the chimp genome aligns with humans. Why aren't we morphologically more similar to gorillas? Why do we retain genetic resemblance with gorillas if we allegedly separated some five million years before our so-called separation from chimps?

Rather than comparing just the similarities among genomes, what is more important is *how* the genes are used and *what* genes are expressed. In other words, it is not about gene *type* but gene *usage*. What tells a gene how and when to express? And, there are over three thousand known human/chimp genes that cause structural *differences* in the two species. Humans, for example, do not have the cell surface sugar gene (GL-Nuer) that is found in mammals, which leads to a totally different brain function. The FOXP2 gene, which determines language capacity, is a different shape in humans than in chimps; the form, which is as important as composition, could not have been acquired through a gradual modification of preexisting systems under natural selection (Rana and Ross 2015). The big changes resulting from just one expressed gene show it is not just similar genes that are important but those that are different. As Chesterton observed, "To say something is *like* something, such as this dog is *like* that cat, is as much a statement of difference as similarity."

Differences exist in animals with similar genetic sequences that have nothing to do with genes. The human and mouse genomes, for example, share an 80 percent similarity and yet no one says we came from mice. Anthropologist John Marks asserts, "Gene comparison is largely meaningless. Humans and daffodils have a 35 percent similarity yet to say humans are one-third daffodil is ludicrous" (Marks 2003, 29). Natural causes cannot regulate complex networks and sequences of gene interaction to generate the necessary structures. And, random mutation cannot make the demanding changes in gene structure needed to support new biological functions for the simple reason that structure-altering mutations usually result in weakness or disease. There is something else going on and genes do not tell the whole story, another dynamic accounting for the differences in organisms. As one scientist said regarding the human/chimp connection, "Even if the '99%' canard were true, it wouldn't make us 99% chimps any more than a diamond's carbon composition makes it 99% coal."

REVIEW QUESTIONS:

Why is it too simple to say that similar genes alone account for common ancestry and homologous structures among organisms?

What is a favorite argument from genetics that Darwinists use for a common ancestor?

List the problems with a strict, quantitative comparison of genes to prove ancestry with chimps and humans.

Could there be another dynamic, other than genes, that determines the differences in species?

LESSON 10

Fossils as Fuel for Design

OBJECTIVES:

state when and why Darwinists go the fossil evidence to support macroevolution

appraise the Cambrian explosion and the problems surrounding it for a macroevolutionary explanation of life

articulate Darwin's concession if problems of his theory were found in the fossil layers

cite three replies Darwinists give for the problems in the fossil record and present the counter responses

supply reasons why the fossil record best supports top-down design as an explanation for the emergence life

Icebreaker:

To say of what is that it is not, or of what is not that it is, is false; while to say of what is that it is, and of what is not, that it is not, is true.

—Aristotle on the Law of Identity

It is impossible, then, that "being a man" should mean precisely "not being a man"...And it will not be possible to be and not to be the same thing.

—Aristotle on the Law of the Excluded Middle

THE LATE EVOLUTIONIST COLIN PATTERSON once admitted, "Fossils may tell us many things, but one thing they can never disclose is whether they were ancestors of anything else" (Patterson 1978, 133). Fossils are limited in their support of evolution, but Darwinists still lean on paleontology and the fossil record to underwrite their theory. Missing links are hard to come by in the fossil record, in part, because biologists can't agree on the difference between a transition, a variation and a species. We do not observe the processes of the past before our eyes like we can in biology, making fossil interpretation more speculative. If current biological processes really do not vindicate evolutionary mechanisms, fossils are less inclined to do so since they house little DNA and record unrepeatable events of the past. As such, paleontological journals can read more like historical narratives, with creative scenarios filling in the matrix among the hard-core facts of fossils. Fossils are not always the raw material facts for an exact science as are sometimes put forth.

The fossil record's great pantheon of activity comes in the described Cambrian explosion, alleged to begin about 550 million years ago. Ninety-five percent of all known animal phyla emerged in this relatively brief period (geologically speaking) of five to ten million years. After the

middle Cambrian, there is a sharp drop in activity and virtual silence in the fossil record. Preceding the Cambrian, some relatively primitive unicellular organisms appear in the Ediacaran formation of Australia, not related to the Cambrian. The explosion is just that, a sudden unveiling of fully developed life-forms with no trail of descent. Bam, complex creatures appear like shooting stars across the skyline and then disappear.

The Cambrian explosion jams a stick into the spokes of the macroevolutionary machine, the illogic of evolution exposed in its own context. No documented pathways exist among far-ranging phyla *after* the sudden appearance of these life-forms. Nor are there evolutionary transitions or phyletic pathways of descent *before* the explosion. A proliferation of classes should be expected after the explosion if the tree of life is secure. In that relatively short window of time, the fossils appear the same as when they disappear, with no directional changes. However, there is a static stability and existence of animals within the period known as *stasis*. The fossil record reflects the same pattern we see today in living organisms, where animals are born, live within a basic biological boundary, and die off. Even the late Harvard biologist Steven Jay Gould acknowledged that "the extreme rarity of transitional forms in the fossil record persists as the trade secret of paleontology" (Gould 1980, 181). If Darwinian interpretation creates so much mystery, perhaps design clarifies it. Both origin and operational science consistently refute random chance and support the sudden appearance of design.

After careful examination, biochemist Michael Denton found no evidence for transitions on a molecular level and states, "none of the groups traditionally cited by evolutionary biologists as intermediates gives even the slightest hint of a supposedly transitional character" (Denton 1986, 286). To his credit, Darwin acknowledged that the absence of transitional forms creates a major problem for his theory. He wrote in *The Origin of the Species*: "If it could be demonstrated that any complex organ existed which could not possibly have been formed by numerous, successive, slight modifications, my theory would absolutely break down" (Darwin 1964, 189). He thought surely that the "intermediate and transitional links must have been conceivably great" (Darwin 1859, Chap. 9). But 150 years later nothing has been found, not even credible meager evidence for the alleged missing links. One scientist said that we can easily fit all the known "missing links" into a coffin.

Creation scientists have an interesting explanation for the so called Cambrian explosion. With catastrophic evidence in the fossil layer and as well as in Scripture, this explosion of life could easily be interpreted as a detonation of death. The Cambrian explosion is really a mass extinction of irreducibly complex organisms, answerable by sudden creation and catastrophic devastation. If deep time complicates the Cambrian explanation a universal flood, such as that of Genesis 6-8, is a natural and scientifically defensible argument for the brisk elimination of living creatures in the strata layers around the world.

MIDPOINT QUESTIONS:

Are fossils a reliable body of evidence for Darwinists to support evolution? Why or why not?

What is the Cambrian explosion and what is said to have occurred there?

According to Darwinism, what should be present if such a Cambrian explosion occurred?

What does the absence of gradually modified organisms on either side of the Cambrian explosion indicate?

Without the presence of transitional links, what did Darwin admit?

Neo-Darwin paleontologists present three rationalizations to defend the naturalistic formation of life and the problems of transitions. First, they say we have an *imperfect record* of the past, and we need a more thorough account of the fossil profile. But really, how much evidence do we need to establish life from random processes? Forty-two out of forty-three orders have been found, as well as 80 percent of the 329 families in existence. Second, they reply that there has been an *inadequate search* for transitions. Darwin said, "We should not forget that only a small portion of the world is known with accuracy" (Darwin 1872, Chap. 10). Darwin may get a little leeway because he didn't know what we know. But in the century and a half since Darwin, every rock type has been scoured in the search for missing links, often miles below the surface, with zero examples of any transitions. Quartz nodules have even been pried open in the search for any traces of life, and nothing. We have been through thousands of feet of sediment and no links. Fossils are always found in clumps or "nested clusters," themselves separated by gaps. Not only is there an absence of transitional forms, but new fossils have been found that actually

exacerbate the Darwinian problem. The search has actually opened up new unbridgeable gaps in the tree of life!

The third rationalization to the evolutionary problem of the Cambrian explosion is called *punctuated equilibrium*, which was put forth by Steven Jay Gould. He acknowledges the problem of the sudden appearance and stasis of organisms during the Cambrian period, calling it "an embarrassing feature in the fossil record," and "nonevidence for nonevolution" (Gould 1993). In getting around the suddenness leading up to stasis in the fossil record, he proposed that evolution was likely quick (thousands, not millions of years in geological terms) in the pathways *among* major life-forms. Thus, the rapid changes in the links *between* species are not preserved. The small numbers and short time frames of the transitional links caused them to disintegrate, and what we see recorded are the "humps and jerks" in the fossil record. All the visible phyla forms were the slowing-down process or stasis. But the speciation among and between the phyla was the speeding up process, which is thought to be why they are not preserved (Dembski and Wells, 2008).

The problem with Gould's proposal is that "statements about ancestry and descent are not applicable in the fossil record," says Darwinist Colin Patterson (Patterson 1993). Gould's ad hoc argument from silence attempts to explain descent with little molecular evidence, and is another example where science is more like speculation, novel or science fiction. Gould believed that evolution has real mechanisms to explain the sudden arrival of fully formed life forms in the fossil record. And his proliferation of *punctuated equilibrium* is a Marxist doctrine adopted from the Russian revolution decades before, where a sudden revolutionary change to a classless society must be rapid; Marxist political theorists embrace this concept from biology to nourish their political worldview where the pseudo-science of evolution is more of a quest for civil power (Martin 2008, 185). We will see there has not been the time for natural selection to have run through all the combinations of genetic coding for each organism and its transitional links to adapt to their environments. Scientific naturalists will say anything but admit the obvious, that this world is designed. How long will some of these scientists appeal to the veil of the unknown before assenting to the best-known argument for the data?

The sudden appearance of phyla in the fossil layer better reflects top-down design rather than bottom-up speciation, divergence, or modification with descent. Science is about face-value interpretation. If transitions have not been revealed by now, more time and searches will not uncover the transitions needed for a Darwinian categorization of the fossil explosion. One sidebar worth noting is that, as a result of the fossil pursuit, *de-evolution* has actually been observed in nature. If Darwinists insist on the science as they understand it, the more sophisticated cells with a nucleus (eukaryotes) *come before* the simpler cells without a nucleus (prokaryotes) in the geologic strata. This conflicts with the major premise of Darwinism, where organisms were supposed to have evolved from the simple to the complex. All things equal, the Darwinian mechanism prefers simplicity *over* complexity, and there is no reason to account for evolution in complexity-increasing directions (Dembski and Wells 2008).

REVIEW QUESTIONS:

What are three responses Darwinists give for the problems of macroevolution in the fossil record?

How does Steven Jay Gould explain the "Cambrian explosion," and where does it break down?

What does the fossil record actually report in terms of the progression of life-forms?

Why is top-down design more plausible to explain the fossil explosion rather than bottom-up gradual descent?

What is the creation science explanation for the so-called Cambrian explosion?

What agenda could Darwinists have other than science?

Specified Complexity and the Impossibility of Chance Based Life

———— ⊷⊷⊷ ————

OBJECTIVES:

illustrate the concept of specified complexity

clarify how chance-based mechanisms cannot account for the existence of life

state how complex systems evolving through small increments hinder evolution

articulate how the universal probability bound renders chance-based life as an impossible occurrence

ICEBREAKER:

The old argument of design in nature, as given by Paley, which formerly seemed to me so conclusive, fails, now that the law of natural selection has been discovered. We can no longer argue that, for instance, the beautiful hinge of a bivalve shell must have been made by an intelligent being, like the hinge of a door by man. There seems to be no more design in the variability of organic beings and in the action of natural selection, than in the course which the wind blows.

—Autobiography of Charles Darwin

⸺⸺

CELL EXPERT STEPHEN MEYER WRITES, "The term specified complexity is… a synonym for specified information or information content," (Meyer 2009). Complex and immaterial information is integral to the formation of life. If genetic data is one of intelligent design's strongest argument in the Darwin versus design debate, specified complexity may be the best tool to detect it. A sibling of irreducible complexity, specified complexity brings the precision of mathematics to correct the ambiguity of random variation; it renders irreducible complexity quantifiable and chance a non-issue. The premise is that design is detected in nature if events and systems are not just improbable but are also complex and patterned. An event

has to be intricate and specified in a detectable pattern by means of information.

Simply observing *complexity* in nature is not enough to identify a designer because some things are randomly complex, such as a complicated but unpatterned wind-blown rock formation in the desert. Likewise, *patterns* are not enough to detect a designer since simple patterns occur in nature all the time, such as the ripples in the sand on a beach. (Nature can produce patterns but it cannot produce information). Biological systems occurring in nature by random chance are tantamount to scattering a bunch of scrabble pieces all over the floor and expecting an intelligent piece of literature to form; there may result a complex assemblage of letters, but without a message there is no arrangement. The secret to arguing for a designer through the empirical method is finding evidence in natural systems that are patterned, complex, *and* specified. Specified complexity identifies natural functions and biological organisms that are impossible to be brought about as the result of chance alone. When identified in nature, specified complexity shows that biological organisms coming into existence as products of design is the only logical conclusion.

Specified complexity works like this. If one shoots an arrow from a bow at a large wall, wherever it landed would be considered random chance. Likewise, if one painted a bull's-eye around the arrow on the wall *after* the shot, still no design is ascribed since there was no predictive element to the shot. But if a bull's-eye is placed on the wall before

the shot and an arrow hits the center of the target, design would be concluded because the target was specified, predicted and intended. The existence of the bull's-eye specifies a rejection region on the part of the wall that is *not* painted, as well as a targeted region with intentionality inside the circle. In like manner, the countless functions of the smallest biomolecular systems efficiently hitting their targets every time within the cell, whether it is in the making of amino acids or DNA transcription, is the precision of specified complexity. From the integrated parts in the bacterial flagellum to the precise information content of DNA, naturalistic explanations are insufficient to explain life since they are specified in irreducibly complex ways (Dembski 2004).

Sometimes Darwinists will deny the randomness charge with phrases such as, "Evolution is less about randomness since natural selection is really a sifting of the effects of randomness." But that begs the questions: Where did the life-forms, biological systems and DNA come from that could be sifted in the first place? What about the law of the conservation of information, which is antagonistic to the imagined generating processes of mutation? Natural selection has no knowledge of the future and can only arrange what is given at the moment, with no forward-looking, targeted regions in molecular organisms. Random chance has neither prior knowledge of a system nor a specified pathway that needs to be hit to maintain or upgrade species. If chance retained foresight, evolution would have teleological powers of planning the theory says it does not possess. Random variation is not a prescriptive or generative engine as Darwinists so require; it merely describes probabilities through statistics. Dembski and Wells expose the problem of randomness in natural selection:

> Natural selection, as an instant gratification mechanism, has no capacity for standardizing the products of evolution. Yet without standardization, what evolution can manufacture and innovate becomes extremely limited...In the absence of goal directedness, evolution faces a number of daunting hurdles that render the formation of irreducibly complex molecular machines highly improbable... (Dembski and Wells 2008, 188, 182).

If businesses or organizations operated like organisms under a Darwinian framework, where there was no capacity to anticipate or plan for the future, they would cease to exist. To be sure, some scientists now admit that life appears to have purpose beyond current survivability or utilitarian roles. But how does life get information and complexity from random processes, without forward looking intelligence to establish that purpose? Just because we do not see the shooter of the arrow, we conclude design because of how often biological systems hit their targets with precise information. Aristotle said, "It is absurd to suppose that ends are not present because we do not see an agent deliberating."

Midpoint Questions:

What is specified complexity?

Using the concept of an arrow and a bull's-eye, how does specified complexity work in detecting design?

How are the Darwinian mechanisms of natural selection acting on random variation incongruent with specified complexity?

Wed to chance-based mechanisms, atheistic biologist Richard Dawkins says in his book *Climbing Mount Improbable* that the way to overcome the overwhelming odds of apparent complexity in the universe is to chip away at it with baby steps. He says, in effect, that evolution by chance is possible by breaking down complex systems into small subsets or functions. When Dawkins acknowledges the apparent specified complexity in the universe, he pivots and minimizes chance as a major mechanism. Along with the problems of cooption covered earlier, the solution he suggests of a shortened sample set by chance actually creates more problems than it solves. Chance, even in small steps, is still chance.

If generating life were broken down into smaller units or processes to make chance more likely, sample sets based on probability tables result in less order when shortened. If one tosses a coin one hundred times, more chaotic patterns and unspecified intricacy would result than by tossing it one million times. It is only when activity processes are extended that they result in probabilities becoming centered around predictable and patterned averages. Small steps and slight modification decrease the repetition needed for biological systems to hit their targets and increase the probability problems for Darwinian chance. Even if longer random sample sets were possible in nature, chance still flows into patterned averages, displaying it as subordinate to the arrangements of design. Moreover, the use of a coin (or any prop) illustrating the effects of chance still has a designer tossing the coin to get the averages!

Scripture also exemplifies random chance as subordinate to the complexities of intelligent design. Before the wicked king Ahab of the northern kingdom of Israel went into a battle, a prophet predicted his death from a vision (1 Kings 22:20–28). Not convinced of the prophecy, the king went to war anyway and 1 Kings 22:34 says, "Someone drew his bow *at random* and hit the king of Israel between the sections of his armor." An amazing random shot to be sure, on a human level. Was it random when the curtain is pulled back to reveal that the king's death was predicted and specified in battle ahead of time? Sometimes the complexity of quantum physics is brought up to illustrate randomness. But Scripture fills in more detail. Behind the apparent randomness in nature is a designer and quantum dynamics is just the complexity we would expect for an infinite Designer to affect matter and energy. Chance means nothing without a designer. Chance is descriptive, not prescriptive, as life does not organize or operate on its own. Because it is so improbable that the universe came into existence by chance, the only other option is intelligent design. The odds of a Darwin mechanism coordinating successive changes in irreducibly complex biological systems are nil.

The impossibility of natural forces creating life by chance is advanced by the work of theoretical biologist and complex systems researcher Stuart Kauffman. Refuting chance based evolution in its own arena of deep time, he contributed to what is known as the universal probability bound of the universe, which is 1 in 10 to the 150th power. Based on the estimated amount of resources or particles in the universe, the universal probability bound is the threshold under which any event in the universe (including chance-based life) has not had enough time to run through all of the combinations of occurrences since the purported big bang. It is the figure against which chance-based mechanisms are powerless by Darwinian processes. In other words, the universal probability bound is the upper limit on the number of physical events that could possibly have occurred in the observable universe since its inception, which includes the maximum rate per second at which transitions in physical states can occur. According to one expert, "The universe is too small a place to generate specified complexity by sheer exhaustion of possibilities…[and an event] cannot be rendered reasonably probable even if all available probabilistic resources in the known universe are brought to bear against it" (Dembski 2004, 118, 117).

How does this concept apply when we factor in the reputed Cambrian explosion in the fossil record? We have seen that these fauna strata levels could be better classified as *information explosions*, because the majority of known animal phyla occurred in this segment. The organisms that emerged there required fifty cell types, in contrast to the five cell types for the most advanced organisms immediately preceding the explosion. Even with Gould's proposal of "humps and jerks" in the fossil record, there still was not enough time for chance to run through all the complex combinations of biological systems to arrive at forty-five more cell types during the fossil explosion than existed just prior to the eruption. A 4.5 billion year old earth notwithstanding, the universal probability bound of the universe says there is not enough time for chance to create even a simple new protein, much less a new cell. (There is an estimated 37 trillion cells in the human body, each as complex as a city with its moving parts and assignments!). The probability of an event, such as all the available proteins needed to make just *one* biological system (much less one cell) coming together in the right combination of DNA nucleotide sequences is zero. An event goes from improbable to impossible when its chance of happening becomes too small. Though he wouldn't concede to design advocates, even Dawkins admitted: "The more statistically improbable a thing is, the less can we believe that it just happened by blind chance. Superficially the obvious alternative to chance is an intelligent Designer" (Dawkins 1982, 130).

The impossibility of biochemical organisms generated by chance is further evidence by genetic studies. Nobel laureate Francis Crick revealed that the genetic code could not undergo significant evolution. The reason is any change in codon assignments (a genetic unit that assigns the correct amino acids to the correct proteins), would lead to catastrophic changes in the amino acids of every polypeptide in the cell. Though amino acids (the building blocks of life that form proteins) are ordered by their respective codons in tangible ways, no code has ever been observed to materialize by mere physical processes. Only design can fashion pre-existing complex codes to appear at the same time as the physical process. (Lesson 13 shows how physical processes alone cannot explain the formation of codes). Because the genetic code displays few alterations and is durable enough to withstand errors, it must have been universal, optimized and standardized from the beginning. It could not have developed or evolved by natural selection, a powerful argument for design.

Though a changing genetic code is mandatory for evolution, there are other reasons that make such a change impossible. Though debated, it is worth noting the calculations of the late University of California, Berkley biophysicist Hubert Yockey. He estimated that natural selection would have to explore 1.4×10^{70} different genetic codes in nature to discover the universal code. The problem is, even with the deep time necessary for evolutionary theory, only 6.3 x 10^15 seconds have transpired since the alleged inception of life 3.86 billion years ago. This means natural selection would have to sift 10^{55} random codes per second to find the one that is universal (Yockey 1992). In other words, there has not been enough time for natural selection to have run through all the combinations of codes to find the one that is universal, which seems to have just appeared. Some intelligent design advocates and creationists have found flaws in Yockey's postulations. At minimum, the calculation displays the problems that surface with post evolutionary descent and organisms repeatable by chance processes with the suggested amount of time available. In the case of the cytochrome c oxidase protein pump mentioned in Lesson 7 (which evolutionists point to as an example of cooption), researchers have found that because it is so rare not enough time has existed for randomness to have found it by chance. Only a designer, and not randomness, can intention life through the dispensing of information.

Review Questions:

Why is Richard Dawkins's argument for complex systems forming through smaller steps untenable?

From probability statistics, how is random chance still subordinate to design?

What is the universal probability bound of the universe and why is the fossil explosion impossible by chance?

Why does the universal probability bound render it impossible for chance-based mechanisms to sift through all of the combinations of proteins necessary for life?

Why is the genetic code considered an established universal standard and not developed by natural selection?

Soup or Sludge? The Thin Evidence for Chemical Evolution

———∞∞∞———

OBJECTIVES:

define abiogenesis

explain the need for Darwinian scientists to appeal to chemical evolution for the origin of life

outline Oparin's prebiotic soup hypothesis as well as his assumptions about the origin of life on early earth

list the fatal objections to the prebiotic soup proposition

Icebreaker:

Scientists gathered at a conference to talk about the latest discoveries.

The conversation turned to the topic of God, and one said, "Look, the list of our accomplishments is long and we're so advanced we don't need God anymore. Why don't we challenge God to a man-making contest?"

They all agreed and elected one of the scientists to approach God. The scientist went to the top of a hill and said to God, "We've cloned animals, and we're on the verge of cloning humans. We just don't think we need you and would like to challenge you to a man-making contest."

"A man-making contest?", God replied. "You're on, and I will even let you go first."

The scientist bent down to grab a handful of dirt when God interrupted, "Hold it. Get your own dirt!"

—⊶∞⊷—

University of California, Berkeley biophysicist Hubert Yockey said that, "The belief that life on earth arose spontaneously from non-living matter, is simply a matter of faith in strict reductionism and based entirely on ideology" (Yockey 1992). As atheistic ideologists, evolutionists try to account for the changes in organisms once they somehow began. Furthermore, they are compelled to offer an explanation as to how life started by materials only. Though chemical evolution tries to fit that bill, its postulations are less than inspiring and plausible.

Microbiology is an *operation* science where we can currently observe the processes of life in real time, while chemical evolution is an *origin* science that studies past events. If evolutionary microbiology is laden with fatal errors under its current worldview assumptions, chemical evolution is even more speculative. Not only is there an absence of macroevolution in the processes we currently see, the problems compound when we project onto the past a scenario for life's origins through material means only. Chemical evolution is that attempt to describe the sequence of chemical steps under fixed laws by which life might have first formed on the early earth in a closed system. It heroically tries to explain the existence of the first cell from nonliving matter, or what is known as abiogenesis. According to the Law of Biogenesis, only life can beget life; that is, life cannot proceed from nonlife (abiogenesis). How was this primary law of biology violated by mere natural processes to allow for abiogenesis in the first place? Though we do not see abiogenesis today, it obviously must have taken place at least once in the past, most certainly by a designer rather than by a random collision of molecules. One researcher writes,

Evolutionists likewise have assumptions. They take many necessary steps for granted in the molecules-to-man model. In other words, evolutionists assume that non-living chemicals gave rise to the first living cells which, in turn, mindlessly and randomly evolved into ever and ever more complex forms of life. There are no scientific experiments to prove the molecules-to-man scenario. Molecules-to-man is not scientifically testable or experimentally verifiable...(Martin 2008, 43).

Nonetheless, scientific materialists are relentlessly committed to explaining how life came from nonlife apart from design, and the predominant framework of today was sketched out by a Russian biochemist. In the 1920s, Alexander Oparin formed a theory known as Oparin's hypothesis, which still shapes modern thinking with its term "prebiotic soup." The overall scenario goes like this. In the early earth, the atmosphere turned the oceans into a hot soup of chemicals and molecules. Simple chemicals combined after hits and misses to form organic compounds such as amino acids. These, in turn, formed microscopic clumps through chemical reactions caused by lightning and cosmic rays in the seas, resulting in virus-like particles that led to the first cells. Scientific materialists do not appeal to chance alone in this astounding, random sequence of molecular collisions but rely on determinism, natural laws, and some internal tendency in matter toward self-organization (which will be addressed in the next lesson).

The *protocells* that formed in this chemical ocean, however, require many assumptions in Oparin's theory. First, there had to be an abundance of hydrogen in the atmosphere and an absence of oxygen (oxygen combines easily with other elements and destroys organic matter). Second, the energy that formed the microscopic clumps of organic compounds, such as cosmic rays, also didn't destroy them. Third, since DNA is required for the organization of matter, both *information* and the physical mechanism coevolved simultaneously and gradually. Fourth, the process was a long one that occurred over hundreds of millions of years (which seems believable until the details are probed). The Miller/Urey experiment in the 1950s seemingly upholds this chemical evolution scenario, where simple amino acids (the building blocks of proteins) were formed in a controlled environment of placed substances. With its hydrogen, ammonia, methane, water vapor contents and other similarities to earth's atmosphere, the planet Jupiter was once envisioned as a locus of experimentation to validate this grand scheme.

MIDPOINT QUESTIONS:

Why is an origin science like chemical evolution more speculative than the operation science of biology?

What is abiogenesis?

What is Oparin's hypothesis and what are the assumptions embedded into it?

The fatal errors of self-organization in some chemical ocean surface when the details are examined. The first problem is that the energy that attracts in self-organization also breaks apart and separates molecules, making self-organization a two-edged sword. Oceans do not preserve organic matter since the turbulence of watery environments hinders the formation of biomacromolecules. Second, Oparin's narrative requires the absence of oxygen for life to form because oxygen immediately destroys chemical organization, especially organic matter. But the best evidence shows that oxygen was *always* present in the early atmosphere. In the same vein, there was no hydrogen in the atmosphere at that time, as required by Oparin's assertion, because it was too light. Third, we find no geologic evidence for a prebiotic accumulation of organic matter in strata layers. If so many "natural" trials and errors of molecules occurred, there should be preserved a "fossil soup" of prototypes and experimental models somewhere, just as there are the major animal phyla preserved in the fossil explosion. But there is no fossil soup outbreak where there should be plenty of opportunity for one to be found in the clay deposits at life's evolutionary origin.

The fourth problem with self-organization is that any chemical reaction proposal to the formation of life requires energy. In the case of chemical evolution, haphazard lightening or cosmic rays are the proposed sources. However, directly controlled energy would be needed if it were even possible to begin the process of life in deep time, which the early earth didn't have. The Miller/Urey

experiments of the 1950's used directly controlled light to form the building blocks of life (amino acids) which seemingly supports the Oparin hypothesis. But an early earth, under evolutionary assumptions, could only have slapdash energy sources; modern controlled environments were nothing like a requisite early earth chaotic environment.

The fifth problem with self-organization is that Miller/Urey randomly produced both left-handed and right-handed amino acids. But only left-handed amino acids (known as homochirality) can produce life. These amino acids are arranged and folded in very specific ways to build proteins and it is an enormous step to go from random amino acids to the building of complex proteins that perform the work in a cell. The reactions that take place on a small level do not work with compounds and incredibly complex biomacromolecules. In other words, amino acids do not readily react with one another and highlight the huge jump from these to complex molecules like proteins and DNA. In addition to the proteins it forms, DNA itself is a three-dimensional tertiary structure, and its shape is just as important as its chemical ingredients in forming life. As Cambridge geophysicist Meyer says, "Because of its three-dimensional specificity, one protein cannot usually substitute for another" (Meyer 2009). *Not only are the right chemicals required, but also the correct structure and configuration. The correct form and not just the right elements is a mystery that self-organization cannot adequately explain.*

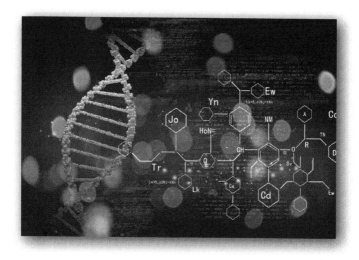

The impossibility of such an early prebiotic cocktail is supported by further analysis. Subsequent experiments based on Miller/Urey always end in a "prebiotic sludge" and not a soup, resulting in their abandonment as a defense of the chemical ocean hypothesis. Though textbooks still mention Miller/Urey, any credible scientist discards the experiments. Ground-breaking research shows how the mystery of DNA, as an immaterial information bearing system, is required to bridge the gap from non-living chemicals to living cells. These issues don't even begin to describe the enormity of the problem of life formed in an early chemical ocean (Dembski and Wells 2008, 214-234). Biochemist Michael Denton writes, "Considering the way the prebiotic soup is referred to in so many discussions of the origin of life as an already established reality, it comes as something of a shock to realize that there is absolutely no positive evidence for its existence" (Denton 1986). The average person cannot fathom how impossible it is to jump from inorganic to complex biomacromolecules that house information. The layman cannot grasp how unattainable it is for parts to drift off and become integrated in a new and tightly fitted biological system in cooption (while the system is maintaining its current functions). Yet evolutionary literature still says "it's a short step to solving some of the mysteries of speciation...and how complexity and diversity can be built up out of very simple beginnings" (Hayden, *Smithsonian* 47). Simple beginnings and irreducible complexity are mutually exclusive concepts.

The chaos theory of chemical evolution is the best that reductionistic science can come up with for the origin of life. It is too easy for researchers to hide behind poor theories about the unknown and say, "Well, we just don't know yet; we have to wait and see." Scientists will never stop examining, but science is also about the best explanation for the data as we have it now. Design has more evidence than Darwinism even though evolution is inserted into textbooks and called established fact. A refutation of chemical evolution is an automatic argument for design, as there are no other options. Design is not against new discovery or expanding the boundaries of thought as we know them; it is a workable theory that has the capacity to welcome new data without upsetting its major principles. With such a clean track record, design advocates are confident any future discoveries will be consistent with, and fall under, the umbrella of a design framework for life's origins. As the DNA mystery will reveal, design is not only preferred but is necessary for the origin of life.

Review Questions:

What conditions of the early earth refute a prebiotic assembly of molecules?

What did the Miller/Urey experiment really produce?

If there was any truth to Miller/Urey, how would the experiments still fall under a design label?

If a fossil explosion has been found, why hasn't a "fossil soup" been found by now?

How is structure just as important as chemical composition in early macromolecules?

Why is it poor science to hide behind the unknown rather than admit the more plausible design inference?

DNA: A Classic Chicken-or-Egg-Scenario

—❦—

OBJECTIVES:

show how information-oriented DNA is required at the source of life

discuss the paradox of DNA and the problem it presents to the scientific materialist

use DNA as a prime tool in the design argument for the origin of life

ICEBREAKER:

Question: What was the highest mountain before Mount Everest was ever discovered?

Answer: Mount Everest. Like the scientific method it-self, we don't determine our own truth, we discover it. Truth is anterior and not something the mind alone forms.

Reality is independent of the mind. Truth or knowledge exist in the mind when the mind agrees with, confirms, or corresponds with independent reality.

—Mortimer Adler

THE DESIGN OF THE MICRO-BIT digital system is central to the advancement of the modern era. Amazingly, digital technology is also central for life in biological systems. Information codes are integral to the formation of life and all codes are programmed by designers. Genetic data is one of intelligent design's strongest argument in the Darwin versus design debate. Even Richard Dawkins acknowledged that, "A gene is a long sequence of coded letters, like computer information" (Dawkins 2013).

Yet the question remains. If genes are comprised merely of phosphates, sugars, nitrogen, oxygen and hydrogen, how does nature bring about intelligence-rich biological structures in a closed system of inert chemicals? The information of DNA is comprised of but not reduced to elements, just like a newspaper consists of dead trees yet houses information from an intelligent source. (Depending on the newspaper, there are varying levels of intelligence!). Where does the information system of DNA come from in the chemical evolution of life? Alexander Oparin assumed that "DNA is the end product of metabolism, and the nucleus is the dustbin of the cell" (Evolution News and Views, 2012). But we know DNA is not an end-product; it is cocreated with the primary functions of life in the cell. Though DNA is one of the great mysteries of life, it has to be present in the earliest life-forms for life to work. Oparin got the order wrong, and DNA is a dagger in the heart of Darwinism.

There is little difference between the dirt under our feet and the matter in our bodies. The difference between organic and inorganic properties is how they are arranged. In what way matter is prescribed requires information, and DNA enters origin-of-life scenarios as the information-bearing system. Information is a profoundly strange phenomenon in that it is empirically verifiable in its message and mediums, but it is so highly complex that it transcends material explanations. The nucleotide bases of A, C, T, and G are chemical letters that encode proteins in the cell through which cells function. To say natural processes alone produce information is akin to monkeys

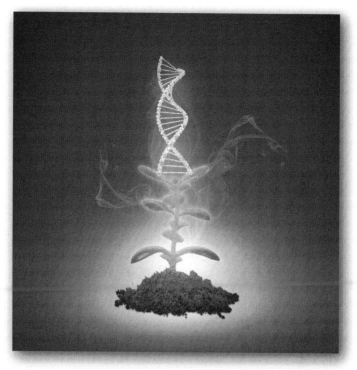

typing at random on a keyboard. The monkeys will not produce anything more than a few random words, much less a meaningful sentence or a valuable classic of literature. Likewise, the presence of chemical letters does not inherently mean there is a message in the genome. *What is profound is that the cell can discern the difference between a random assemblage of letters and a meaningful message in nature.* If you were to walk through a remote national forest and saw the letters Bill + Suzie carved into a tree, you would never attribute this to chance. A similar conclusion resides with DNA as a chemical code, where the information is not a random result of the costructure that houses it. How can DNA, as a chemical compound, precisely designate where the amino acids should form and which proteins to arrange?

If matter is profoundly arranged by a chemical alphabet that is cocreated with the production of the system, where did the precise information magically appear from? If no naturalistic mechanism has the power to generate relevant information, how can mere natural forces bridge the gap between the organic and inorganic worlds? The answer is found only through abstract information, the physical/immaterial interface, as this is what shapes matter into designed structures. The design found in nature through information indicates that nature is unable to account for everything in nature, and DNA proves information cannot be derived merely from natural forces. Information can only stem from intelligence.

MIDPOINT QUESTIONS:

What is DNA?

What is the difference between the dirt under our feet and the matter in our bodies?

If DNA is required for life, how does its presence contradict theories of self-organization?

What is the problem with natural causes having the ability to generate information?

The great paradox in the formation of life is that DNA is a message-bearing medium and an information coding system. How could an extremely complex message-producing information system arise through natural causes? How is the material realm infused with the domain of the immaterial? From a reductionist standpoint, DNA is a conundrum. DNA is needed to create new cells, yet new cells are created with the DNA, a classic chicken-or-egg scenario. DNA carries a message that tells a cell what kinds of proteins to make and when to make them. But if DNA carries a message, then the message cannot be an outgrowth of the medium. DNA is communication and cannot merely be a product of chemicals, just as the words on this page do not arise from ink and paper (or pixels and circuit boards in the case of Kindle readers). DNA is comprised of chemicals but is not reduced to them. *The problem of how chemistry can produce information is resolved if DNA is the product of design.* Interestingly, DNA physically disintegrates when removed from its cell, validating the fact that information cannot be explained by physical processes alone (Dembski and Wells, 2008).

Since passive, inert matter needs information to be organized, origin is as much about information as merely prebiotic chemicals. Chemistry is not the source of the information because the essential elements of the complex DNA molecule are pre-organic carbon, nitrogen, hydrogen, and oxygen atoms arranged in extremely precise ways. The backbone of the double helix is simply a polymer with an alternating sugar and phosphate sequence. And the nucleotide bases (the building blocks of DNA) are made up of a nitrogen base, as well as a sugar and a phosphate group. DNA itself is arranged precisely so that it can code for functions in the cell in precise ways. Though information is comprised of chemistry, chemistry is only the carrier of information which then acts on matter to give it form and arrangement in very particular ways. *Chemistry only provides the medium for life, but the information it carries cannot be reduced to it.* This relationship is fundamental to an understanding of the world, and manmade machines provide a good analogy. An automobile is made from metal and plastics, but nothing useful arises unless they are arranged with detailed instructions from a designer. DNA shows that information was embedded into life from the beginning.

Where does the information that is laced in, and formed by, the elements come from? Information is intelligence. A designer anticipated the varied selective pressures from the environment and equipped species with volumes of information which can be selected for the purposes of survival and adaptation. As materials need information, intelligence is the most plausible explanation for life's origins. Design, intelligence and information are related notions and biological information is the advantage intelligent design brings to the origin-of-life model. The dearth of substantial explanation for the information-rich chemical language raises credibility issues for all of evolutionary theory. French evolutionary biologist Pierre Paul Grasse disturbed the reductionist community when he said: "It is

possible that in this domain biology, impotent, yields the floor to metaphysics" (Grasse 1977, 477). As an immaterial information bearing system, DNA shows that he couldn't have been more correct.

Review Questions:

What is the paradox of DNA and the chemicals it is comprised of? Why does a reductionist have a greater struggle with origins?

What example from manmade machines illustrates the problem on a molecular level?

If information is intelligence and life needs information, why is design rather than chance the better explanation for the existence of life?

The Fallacy of Biological Self-Organization

———⊗⊗⊗———

OBJECTIVES:

cite examples Darwinists give to support self-organization

refute the properties of crystal growth as support for the spontaneous generation of life

itemize the weakness and irrelevance of the Miller/ Urey experiment

articulate the problem of natural laws as they relate to life's origins

detail the punctured-cell lab test that refutes chemical evolution

Icebreaker:

The morbid logician seeks to make everything lucid but ends up making everything mysterious. The mystic allows one thing to be mysterious and everything else becomes clear.

—G.K. Chesterton

Since therefore falsehood alone is contrary to truth, it is impossible for the truth of faith to be contrary to the principles known by natural religion.

—Thomas Aquinas

RICHARD DAWKINS ONCE SAID, "EVOLUTION has been observed. It's just that it hasn't been observed while its happening" (Dawkins 2004). So, evolution has been observed but it hasn't? If evolution hasn't been observed while it's happening, perhaps mutation is *not* the engine of macro-evolutionary change. With life spawning all around us, how reliable is a theory when it is not testable nor observed in real time? Leading Harvard evolutionary scholar Steven Jay Gould was even more candid: "to preserve our favored account of evolution by natural selection we view our data as so bad that we never see the process we profess to study" (Gould 1977, 14). If the present aspects of macroevolution are not observable, what about a hollowed-out diagram of self-organization in a chemical ocean?

There are only two options for the origin of life, chance or design. The design of information brings a certain logic to the subject of origins, but the dearth of evidence compounds the evolutionary problem exponentially. For a world reduced only to atoms, chance demands a specific material sequence of x's and o's, where self-organization is a necessary component of chemical evolution. Darwinists accuse design advocates of assuming a priori first principles, such as an unverifiable intelligence source. However, what do Darwinists assume? Preexistent physical laws and determinism? Eternal matter? If the first living cell is untestable and evolution from molecule to man is unobservable, evolution is a huge faith based system.

Darwinists never adequately answer the question, "Why is there something rather than nothing?" With no proof, they assume the less plausible dynamics of self-organization and self-reproduction in a closed system. Self-organization is a concept that easily sticks in the mind of the uninitiated and sounds plausible because we have all observed inanimate objects attract, like a magnet pulling a nail. There seems to be some internal property in matter to self-assemble and another example often brought up is

crystal growth, where atoms aggregate in orderly fashion on a growing cluster. But the problems of self-organization are as great as any other point in an evolutionary framework of life.

Self-organization such as crystal growth is confined to the secondary causes of inert chemicals, which is nothing close to the self-replication of functionally integrated biological molecular systems. Life requires the x factor of information, which channels and maintains growth through organic membranes. It is impossible for the Darwinian mechanism of chance to generate an assortment of biomacromolecules, and then for these to become arranged into functionally integrated biological systems. The Miller/Urey experiments show that if self-organization were even possible, irrelevant tars and melanoids result;

gradual replication has interfering cross-reactions. What nature selects in pre-organic beginnings, through secondary causes and fixed laws, results in organically inert dead ends.

When it comes to organic properties, there is actually an inherent prebiotic resistance against self-organization. Amino acids, for example, react with sugars that prevent the formation of DNA. Intelligent causes generate information, while natural causes only transmit it. To say that natural forces can generate the specified complexity of DNA is tantamount to saying that Scrabble pieces have the ability to arrange themselves or self-organize into meaningful sentences on a table. The secret to the origin of life is not in chemicals but in information, where coded information is *not* prebiotic. If life comes from nonlife (abiogenesis), it is not through strict random processes.

Adapting organisms never end up with more information than they started with in DNA sequences. This phenomenon, called the law of the conservation of information, is another fatal blow to Darwinism. When biologists explore biological configuration space in genomes, they always depend on *preexisting* information. Evolutionary processes do not create the information required for success from scratch, and natural processes, including any tendency of matter toward self-organization, cannot generate the required information necessary for life (Dembski and Wells 2008).950

Midpoint Questions:

Why does self-organization sound plausible to the uninitiated?

How is self-organization necessary for a Darwinian explanation of the origin of life?

Why is crystal growth an inadequate example of self-organization in biomacromolecules?

If information is a hallmark of design, how can natural forces give credence to information?

Without a designer, the self-organization of molecules is subject only to physical laws. But where do natural laws come from? Are these also self-organized? How is determinism sufficient to account for the origin of life? What is the dynamic that continually overcomes the second law of thermodynamics in nature, where things left to their own devices go from a state of order to disorder or some equilibrium? Natural laws actually work against the origin of life in the *prebiotic soup*, as natural forces seek to break up and consume macromolecules and raw materials. Even in the Miller/Urey experiments of the 1950s, Darwinists leave out the fact that the amino acid building blocks never spontaneously arranged themselves; the experiments were put together by a designer. Information-rich structures limited the results of self-organization as tars and other useless materials were created instead. Unless material processes overcome daunting odds, they are crushed by natural laws. Upward complexity from spontaneous generation is unachievable. If some faith is required in any philosophy of science, the design in nature requires less faith than chance theory. The following experiment illustrates the impossibility of self-organization and points to another dynamic in the origin of life:

> Take a clean, sterile [test tube]. Place into it a small amount of sterile salt solution, known as a buffer, at just the right temperature and pH. Place into the buffer a living cell, but puncture it with a sterile needle so that its contents leak out into the solution... You now have all the molecules needed to make a living cell—not just the building blocks, but all the fully assembled macromolecules such as DNA and proteins. Moreover, you have them in just the right proportions, under just the right conditions, and without any interfering substances. Yet, despite all such efforts to facilitate the transition from non-life to life, the molecules will not form into a living cell—no matter how long you wait or what you do to them (Dembski and Wells 2008, 232).

REVIEW QUESTIONS:

What explanation do Darwinists provide for the origin of natural laws? How do these laws militate against the formation of life?

Where does the Miller/Urey experiment fail in explaining life's origins?

What repeatable lab test sticks a nail in the coffin of self-organization?

Could there be another dynamic other than random causes and natural laws that better explains the existence of life?

From an Intelligent Designer to the God of the Bible

————⊗∞⊗————

THE THEORY OF EVOLUTION IS everywhere, radiating into our thoughts from early childhood. Lies entombed within the theory are laid down in a matrix of scientific concepts and discernment is needed to whisk away truth from error. If we say to someone so conditioned that "Jesus is Lord," a person may well respond, "That's fine for you, but I am a Darwinist and scientific atheist." How do we answer this? Skeptics in western nations may need reasons if they are to be persuaded to the veracity of the Christian God.

No New Thought Today

Though we live at the pinnacle of technology the world has ever known, the arrogance in contemporariness deems us superior to all generations before us (whatever the nature of that superiority is). Progressivism is fed by evolutionary thought where man gets upgrades as time passes. But no matter how advanced we think we are, we have not solved the problem of mortality and there is no new thought today. Just about everything has been thought of and our era of technological advancement is really horizontal knowledge built on foundations of thought already laid. Interestingly, the ancient Greek word for *technology* is also the word for *design*. Throughout its history, the world has operated on the different philosophies from the ancients, depending on its phase and emphasis. Platonism held that because things have an ethereal prototype or form somewhere, truth is not something we determine since their essences cannot change. Evolutionists dismiss a fixity of species and deride this most famous theory from philosophy because distinct *forms* militate against their belief that life blends seamlessly from one transitional form into another. Evolutionary biologist Richard Dawkins calls essentialism the "dead hand of Plato" and the "tyranny of the discontinuous mind" (Dawkins 2014). But it could be argued that the hairball of modification with descent, with its seamless fluidity, is what clogs up the categories and definitions. As one prominent evolutionist conceded, "The theory of evolution had done more harm than good to biological systematics" (Patterson 1993).

In Epicurean philosophy, the goals of life are the pursuit of pleasure and the avoidance of pain, with an emphasis on intellectual pleasure. Epicurus (300 B.C.) was an atomist who projected modern natural selection and spontaneous generation, believing natural forces alone gave rise to organisms. He also propounded the survival of the fittest where the remaining organisms propagated themselves. Hedonism, a form of Epicureanism, believes in the pursuit of as much pleasure as possible and complements naturalistic notions like Stoicism, where reality is amoral in nature. The atomism of Democritus and Heraclitus reduced existential reality to small indivisible chemical particles, and Empedocles put forth life having begun by chance. As physicist Leon Lederman summarizes, "The history of atomism is one of reductionism-the effort to reduce all the operations of nature to a small number of laws governing a small number of primordial objects" (Lederman 2006).

Evolution has revived some of the naturalistic theories of ancient philosophers, with reductionism and random chance as the two necessary sponsors. The pendulum has swung from the transcendence that characterized the middle ages to an extreme Aristotelian emphasis on the material today, which has all but boxed out any metaphysical explanation for the creation of the world. (An Aristotelian view, in balance, doesn't have to contradict a biblical perspective on creation and the world of matter). The contemporary world has not really invented any new philosophy, and if progressives say they are only "pragmatists" without metaphysical beliefs, that is also an ideology. There is a current trend towards sentimentality and a fascination with ancient wisdom; if progress occasionally means going backwards, an accurate interpretation of our modern world will only be procured by returning to the correct source of wisdom from antiquity, the Scriptures. As C.S. Lewis wrote, "For every new book you read, read an old one; old books tend to correct the errors of the modern era." A theological view of the western world was the dominant rubric for centuries and Christianity is at the core of western thought, progress and the scientific method. Though naturalists have existed from ancient times, modern science at its advent was another medium for affirming the varied mysteries of a Creator. Science did not compete with theology, it complemented it where theology was once "the queen of the sciences, and philosophy her handmaiden."

At the advent of the scientific revolution, the unbeknownst folds of the natural world gave people new occupations of study and mental prosperity. With such employment of mind, men began to bite the hand that fed him and his idolatrous fascination with the material eventually eclipsed God as the foundation for reality. Spurgeon articulates the compulsion, "So I find that a little crawling worm of the earth has more effect upon my soul than the glorious Christ of heaven...simply because earth is near, and heaven is far away" (Spurgeon 1855). Along with notions that positioned the mind as the starting point of knowledge (instead of first things of existence), man gravitated to other philosophies that did not need Him such as existentialism, skepticism, relativism, humanism, subjectivism, and closed-system naturalism. These notions filled the vacuum and became the guiding philosophies of the academic elite, where people did not "turn away from...the opposing ideas of what is falsely called knowledge" (1 Tim. 6:20). Being a Christian, however, is not tantamount to intellectual suicide since theology is the highest in thought. Volumes of philosophy provide no lack of intellectual stimulation for those so inclined and no text of ideology or religion even competes with Scripture on an intellectual level, to say nothing of the incredible spiritual benefits. The insights into the Bible are unending because Scripture is an infinite book from an infinite God.

Chance Is Nothing

In reviving strains of closed-system naturalism from ancient times, Darwinists invoke random variation acting on natural selection as the mechanisms in evolution. Yet the known Darwinian processes do not provide pathways for the independent and complex systems we see in nature. By contrast, intelligent design holds runaway naturalism accountable, as design is detectable *in science* but is not explainable *only by* science. It is one thing to study science; it is quite another to say random chance is responsible for the existence of complex life-bearing forms. Chance is a philosophical claim that goes past the dividing line of science and into metaphysics. Far from being a prescriptive force in nature, chance is descriptive as two authors point out: "Chance' is not a cause. Chance is a word that we use to describe mathematical possibilities. It has no power of its own. Chance is nothing. It is what rocks dream about" (Geisler and Turek 2004, 125). left

Science is as much about philosophy of science as it is about science. Researchers can be less inclined to talk about their philosophies because mental frameworks are ethereal and less empirical. But everybody thinks and the seed of every action is a thought that integrates into a bigger philosophy as to how life is lived. They might portend neutrality in viewing data, but even scientists and academic elites who have the power to shape the cultural conscience have worldviews as to what they believe to be reality. Though a view of reality can be tightly worn like the lenses of glasses, people should think about what they are thinking about to see if the grid through which they filter the data is genuine. Scientific naturalists may question whether there is truth to be found, but they don't doubt the worldview lens through which they interpret data. For those who believe nature is supreme, it can be difficult to convince a naturalist not to believe everything he or she thinks, even if those thoughts are untrue. If nature is supreme, there is no blind reason we shouldn't desire cancer or act on murderous or suicidal thoughts. If the sin nature is natural, why should we admit moral failure?

A philosophy is an immaterial thought process and a testament in itself that the metaphysical exists. With options like reductionism, atheism or theism all scientists have worldviews they bring into the interpretation process of the data. Harvard biologist Richard Lewontin admits that, "we have a prior commitment...to materialism... no matter how counterintuitive...for we cannot allow a Divine

Foot in the door" (Lewontin 1997, 31). At least one evolutionist admits his preconceived ideological bias before he comes to the data. But reductionism, as the secret to ultimate reality, has a host of difficulties as neo-Darwinist Haldane reveals regarding the mystery of the brain:

> It seems to me immensely unlikely that mind is a mere by-product of matter. If my mental processes are determined wholly by the motions of atoms in my brain, I have no reason to suppose that my beliefs are true. They may be sound chemically, but that does not make them sound logically. And hence I have no reason for supposing my brain to be composed of atoms (Haldane, 2001).

The reductionist's dilemma is acute. How can thought, conceptualization, reflection, consciousness, intuition, reason, logic, temptation, vision, guilt and shame be mere products of chemical reactions? If thoughts and reflections are solely the products of electro-chemical reactions, how do we measure the strength of one's will? Where is the love atom? Thinking a thought, using logic to reason through an argument, making a moral judgment, or choosing to do what is right are more than gene expressions. They are participations in things that transcend bodily mechanisms. The brain is the vehicle of thinking and choosing even though thinking and choosing are more than the vehicle and the effects of chemical reactions. "It was the

materialists," writes Chesterton, "who destroyed materialism merely by studying matter" (Chesterton 1931).

If mind precedes matter, how does mind proceed
from matter? Carl Sagan highlights the circular reasoning of closed system reductionism: "The cosmos is within
us; we're made of star stuff. We are a way for the cosmos
to know itself." Yet nature producing mind is a fallacy of
essence. Cabbages may result from the laws of botany but
cabbages cannot produce lectures on the subject. The Gulf
Stream may produce the temperature of the Irish Sea but
the Gulf Stream cannot produce maps of itself, to borrow
Lewis's examples (Lewis 1967, 63). Furthermore, the problems of cooption remain. How do biological systems in bi-
pedal ancestors foresee future needs of the brain and coopt
for more complex faculties? It's reasonable that a designer allocates greater capacities in higher the creatures, which the
gradation in species generally displays. Advanced brains are
repositories for increased mental capacities and if the brain
is the primary physical-metaphysical interface in the body,
only man is made in the image of God with worship abilities. Wrote John Calvin, "the Spirit accommodates Himself
to our capacity" (Calvin 1974, 1:1:249). Modern scientists
may do well to revisit the layered philosophical and theological heritage that led up to modern science and consider
the insights of thinkers such as Aquinas: "Intellectual faculty
[is more than] the actualisation of any organ, as exercising its
activity through that organ" (Aquinas 1905).

Scott S. Chandler

Everyone has metaphysical thoughts. It is impossible for a scientist to separate science from a philosophy of science since no one lives in the world of pure raw data. Assumptions determine conclusions and a scientist still interprets the data (correctly or incorrectly). If one has preconceived notions that all of reality is reduced to materials, that is a philosophical statement. Biologist Richard Dawkins made a metaphysical claim when he wrote, "Darwin made it possible to be an intellectually fulfilled atheist" (Dawkins 1986, 6). If science is about data, why does atheism enter the picture at all? Is that not a preconceived worldview Dawkins brings into the interpretation process? Atheism is intellectually bankrupt and does not have the lexicon to explain the full range of living occurrences. Atheist Peter Atkins says that referencing a Creator is another way of saying we don't have a clue how the universe started, a *god of the gaps* admission of ignorance. He asserts that the Heisenburg uncertainty principle (or chaos theory) of quantum physics proves absolute truth is impossible to know. But if absolute truth is unknowable, why should we believe Dr. Atkin's assertion? The wave/matter/energy mystery may actually reveal the misunderstanding of particle physics from a reductionist point of view. Even though science has been hijacked by those who don't believe in ultimate truth, science is still a means to discover reality. We don't determine our own truth, we discover it. A scientist is a walking contradiction when he or she seeks objective truth through the empirical method, yet insists on being a postmodern relativist who does not believe in absolute truth.

If evolutionary theory is supposed to make no comment on God, how can evolution be defined as "unsupervised" and "impersonal"? Far from an objective assessment about reality, atheism is also an opinion about God and literally means "against theism." Atheism would not subsist without a pre-existing God, a twist on what already exists. It's interesting how often Richard Dawkins mentions God in his writings and conversations, as though God is on his mind beyond what he desires. God is more than a contrivance of the mind or an evolutionary development for the survival value of a community, and Dawkins may be experiencing Romans 1:18-20: "God has made it plain" to him the "creation of the world," and he is irritable because he "suppress[es] the truth" and constantly tries to choke it down. We would ask scientists like Dawkins, "if God doesn't exist, why all the anger and hostility?" God should be just as innocuous as fluffy pink elephants or a moon made of green cheese. Let it slide off your back. But God is not innocuous, and it's not just because a certain subset of humans can't stop mentioning Him. Trying to legislate God out of society by means of scientific atheism is a futile attempt to avoid guilt.

"Religion," said another atheist, "hardens hearts and enslaves minds." How does that work when atheism is now considered the world's third-largest religion, reinforcing its belief system status? That makes Richard Dawkins, according to his colleague, "England's most pious atheist" (Conway-Morris 2003). Most religions do enslave, but only because they distort the viability of the one true religion (which is really a relationship). A relative world needs a reminder that absolutes exist and the *law of singularity* pervades reality; though there are many tennis players, there is only one #1 player in the world. In belief systems, there may be similarities in the peripheries of worldviews but only one is authentic. Paul said there is "one Lord, one faith, one baptism; one God and Father of all" (Eph. 4:5-4). Chesterton phrased the law of singularity this way, "There are many angles by which you fall, only one by which you stand." The major truth claims of all other religions contradict the resurrection and deity of Christ and all religions do not lead to the same place. Godless men cause chaos and chaos theory. If there are many ways to Christ, there is only one way to God and false religions evidence man's collective flee from God's original design, not the pursuit of God.

Though atheistic scientists say they go where the data leads, atheism has religious motives as well, not the least of which is to make sure any theistic implications are boxed out of science. Atheist and chemist Peter Atkins is one such scientist who is vehement against Christianity:

> Someone with a fresh mind, one not conditioned by upbringing and environment, would doubtless look at science and the powerful reductionism that it inspires as overwhelmingly the better mode of understanding the world, and would doubtless scorn religion as sentimental wishful thinking (Atkins 1995, 123.)

Does Atkins mean to imply that scientific atheism is *not* culturally conditioned as a system-wide belief order? Atkins aims too low when he believes reductionism inspires more than theism. Scientific atheists, with a philosophical precommitment against any metaphysical or theistic conclusions, cannot separate their own beliefs from practice. Random chance, a bedfellow of atheism and reductionism, is the basis of origins in evolutionary theory and is as much of a metaphysical claim as any design connotation. To posit that life originated by chance is to make a philosophical and not merely an empirical assertion. "Luck," says biochemist Behe, "is metaphysical speculation; scientific explanations invoke causes" (Behe 1996). Chance contradicts the objectivity of science.

Spilling out in academic terms his own insurrection against the design in nature, Steven Jay Gould went beyond science when he said that if there was a designer, then design should be *optimal*. Since, however, there are apparent bad examples of design in nature then there is no designer. But what does suboptimal mean? If something is asymmetrical but fully functional, is that a bad design? Furthermore, things were created "very good" originally but man's sin caused death and imperfection (Gen. 1:31, 3:6). Gould's logic is a non sequitur, and it is a metaphysical rather than scientific claim to say there is no designer. Evolutionists like Dawkins and Coyne believe that intelligent design is a cover to purvey creationism. But isn't evolution a cover for the dissemination of atheistic chance? As

T.S. Eliott asks, "where is the wisdom in all this knowledge? Where is the life in all this living?"

If Darwinists cannot refrain from metaphysical conclusions in science (such as chance, atheism or a suboptimal designer), what metaphysical conclusions can design advocates make? If empiricism is the height of knowledge and anything beyond is speculative, why is scientific atheism a fair conclusion but design is not? Science is about the pursuit of truth wherever it leads, and if the data leads to closed-system naturalism, so be it. But with DNA, specified complexity and irreducible complexity, closed-system thinking does not settle as the deepest and most satisfying conclusion for the evidence. Life is empty under atheistic naturalism and it is a distortion to look upon a mountain lake at sunset and say, "oh the beauty of what undirected random chance can do." The design in biology points to ultimate reality and an incredibly complex universe is entirely consistent with an infinite God. Science is the process that goes from the known to the unknown and the metaphysical implication of design in the natural world is more plausible. If it is impossible to separate one's philosophy of science from science and a metaphysical implication is inevitable, let us make sure it is the correct philosophy. As Chesterton commented, "The purpose of the intellect is to come to conclusions, or rather to convictions" (Chesterton 1924).

The Only Necessary Being

The insistence on naturalism as all of reality has skewed our view of reality and reductionists may want to reconsider their worldview. Since chance is nothing, a universe by chance means the universe came into being by absolute nothingness. This complete lack of anything and everything, or creation *out of* nothing and *by* nothing, means the universe is self-caused or that the universe has no cause (acaused). In a self-caused universe (causa sui), nothing preexisted and everything that exists never existed. However, a self-caused universe employs circular reasoning where the universe is an outcome of its own presence. The universe cannot cause its own existence and be an effect of that cause at the same time. Nothing cannot create itself because it is not in a position to cause itself until it exists, nor would it have any properties until it came into existence. Also, the universe would be unknowable without attributes to explain its existence since matter is not constrained to produce answers to the questions of its own meaning. "If the whole universe has no meaning," wrote Lewis, "we should have never found out it has no meaning" (Lewis 2001, 39).

Darwin's explanation for the existence of everything only went as far back as the existence of natural laws. But where did these come from? Natural laws cannot coexist with the evolution of the universe and exist independently of it. Total nothingness could not produce consistent observance to the first law of thermodynamics, where the entire amount of matter and energy in the universe is neither decreased nor increased. Nothingness could not provide a generative override of the second law of thermodynamics, where things left to their own devices deteriorate into a state of disorder (or some equilibrium). A universe from nothing cannot teleologically channel life into fixed categories of order with mind staggering complexity. Absolute nothingness cannot be a causal agent, and purpose is not procured in organisms that are sourced in randomness.

In an acausal universe, the universe has no cause. Scientists sometimes use quantum mechanics where subatomic particles seemingly move and reappear without pattern as proof of things perpetually produced out of nothing. But why is there something rather nothing at all? How could things come by nothing, from nothing, out of nothing, and for nothing? If absolute nothingness could spontaneously produce something, scientists would see new somethings arising everywhere. With nothingness, there is no explanation as to why this universe appeared when it did and why it is not a cow, a cabbage, or a clam. (For clarification, the Bible also says the universe came into being *out of* nothing, but not *by* nothing.) Scientists cannot observe quantum particles without affecting their results and quanta seem to know when they are observed. The frustration in not being able to detect or grasp subatomic quanta may be a divine boundary of the wave/matter secret to existence. Perhaps quantum mechanics is just the phenomenon we would expect for a transcendent designer to influence particles in complex and yet unspecified ways.

An acausal universe can also imply an eternal universe where matter is everlasting. But an eternal universe not only contradicts the plethora of evidence for a beginning, it also creates the problem of innumerable secondary causes in nature. An infinite regression of secondary causes going back in time is impossible. Actual infinity does not exist in mathematics and militates against the notion of an eternal universe; if infinity existed, we would never have arrived at today. An endless regression of secondary causes is a statistical impossibility where subordinate causes eventually run out as finite, temporary, changing, unwhole, and derivative within the universe and not beyond it. Temporary secondary causes must point to an original source, a prior unity and a First Cause which even the ancient Greek philosophers reasoned to. Where the universe came from must have arisen from a realm or entity beyond our space and time, not within it. Aquinas declared that "Everything imperfect must proceed from something perfect: therefore, the First Being must be most perfect" (Aquinas 1905, Book 1, 28). The First Cause cannot be coevolving with the universe and be transcendent to it at the same time. The First Cause cannot be both comprised of the material realm and be above it. Therefore, the First Cause must be everything secondary causes are not, such as atemporal, transcendent, nonspatial, eternal, changeless, immaterial, simple, uncaused, omniscient and omnipotent. Interestingly, these traits are elements of "intelligence" as in an Intelligent Designer.

While these attributes do not necessarily prove that the First Cause is the Christian God of the Bible, it so happens these characteristics match what the Scriptures have said about God all along, relayed by the ancients as part of an original design. God is eternal (Gen. 21:32), immaterial (John 4:24), immutable (Mal. 3:6), immortal (1 Tim. 6:16), omnipresent (Ps. 139: 7–10), omniscient (1 Jn. 3:30), omnipotent (Gen. 1:1), infinite (Isa. 66:1), and personal (2 Cor. 6:18). Since things exist that aren't necessary, there must be a being whose existence is necessary. As pure existence, it is impossible for God not to exist and God is the only necessary being who has no cause for Him to be. Every other entity requires support for its existence outside of itself. But God, as His own essence, is the only entity whose basis for existence is in Himself.

When scientists error in their conclusions about the universe, they usually do so in one of three ways: they either conclude an eternal universe, they arrive at creation by random nothingness, or they presume all of reality as comprised of the material. The Bible, as the purest wisdom from antiquity, categorically confronts these three miscalculations in a single verse. Hebrews 11:3 says, "the universe was formed at God's commands." If the universe was "formed," it had a beginning as is not eternal. If *God* formed the universe, then it was not created by nothing or random chance. And if *God* formed the universe, there is more to reality than the world of atoms.

If every effect is generated by a cause and everything that begins to exist has an origin, the universe began to exist by a causal agent. Observation, logic, and empirical verification affirm the premise that the universe began to exist. Even for those who assent to deep time, confirmation of the space-time theorem and the relentless testing on the theory of general relativity point to a caused universe. Though science cannot escape a beginning for the universe, the big bang is an atheistic twist on what Genesis 1:1 has said all along: "In the beginning God created the heavens and the earth." The big bang is a counterfeit to the Genesis account because it is an accidental chance based cataclysmic event that assumes eternal matter and energy. In big bang cosmology, order is brought to eternal matter where a speck managed to overcome its high-density compression through an explosion 8 to 20 billion years ago. Somehow, all the intricate order and design came from this turmoil. Though science generically affirms a beginning, how does order come from a chaotic explosion? Also, the big bang doesn't answer where matter came from, making it subject to the problems of an acausal universe listed above. Since there was no witness to a big bang, faith is required to believe in eternal matter. Only God can form all the contents of the universe out of nothing, and if the Creator caused an original cataclysmic event of creation, it was not an accidental big bang.

God cannot be a cause and an effect of that cause at the same time, and what we see in nature is the exact balance we would expect if God exists. His work is evident yet He himself is transcendent and beyond. Creation is analogue to a designer and the beauty in nature points to a greater God. We do not see God directly under a microscope, but we witness circumstantial evidence and His fingerprints of design everywhere. The artist reserves the right to put a signature on the scene and Hebrews 3:4 says, "God is the builder of everything." As *a posteriori* knowledge, the scientific method validates demonstrations for God's existence where "what is seen was not made out of what was visible" (Heb. 11:3). Aquinas explains:

> When an effect is better known to us than its cause, from the effect we proceed to the knowledge of the cause. And from every effect the existence of its proper cause can be demonstrated, so long as its effects are better known to us; because since every effect depends upon its cause, if the effect exists, the cause must pre-exist. Hence the existence of God, in so far as it is not self-evident to us, can be demonstrated from those of His effects which are known to us (Aquinas 1948).

Naturalists ask if we have ever seen God. But have they ever seen an electron in their origin of life model? Science proceeds from the cause to the effect, and direct observation is not always required to determine something's properties. Since the existence of God (and perhaps some elements of His essence) can be demonstrated by effects, theology is supported by science and science is illumined by theology. The source is better known to us from its works and we see a personal universe. Understanding the First Cause from its effects is the empirical deduction Romans 1:20 indicates, "For since the creation of the world God's invisible qualities—His eternal power and divine nature—have been clearly seen, being understood from what has been made, so that men are without excuse."

What about the existence of other gods? Can there be more than one God? Not only is atheism a logical contradiction, so is polytheism. Multiple gods or a pantheon from which to choose necessitates a prior unity and shows these gods as within the universe and not beyond. Since ultimate reality cannot be both comprised of the created realm and be above it, everything within the universe is separate from God. Therefore, multiple gods cannot be equal nor co-eternal with the ultimate but must be subordinate and caused. Worshipping them confuses the creation with the Creator and demands of the creature only what the Creator can do (Rom. 1:25). Idols are a downgrade and every perceived benefit ascribed to other gods is found only in the Most High God. Settling for an inferior power, which is still subject to the ultimate, will mislead at best and destroy at worst. Though polytheism seems to affirm the spiritual realm, it is another form of atheism.

The notion of other gods also leads to relativism. Abandoning allegiance from God to a subordinate power asserts that God is not absolute. But to make the shift at all means there is a standard that is not relative, by which one judges a better alternative. Something must be undeniable before other options are compared to it and relativism itself is relative and self-defeating. If everything is relative how do we know relativism is true if there is no absolute to measure it by? "Nothing can be relative by itself," write two authors, "and if everything else is relative, then no other relations are real. There has to be something which does not change by which we can measure the change in everything else" (Geisler and Brooks 1990, 276). Rejecting belief in God doesn't negate His reality. To say, "You have your truth and I have mine" goes against the nature of what truth is. Two plus two equals four is true everywhere in the world, for all people at all times, in India as it is in America. We can choose our own beliefs, but we don't choose our own truth.

Where power is not demonstrated, existence is not established. God creates and His resurrection power commenced the antidote for sin in creation. If existence is actual, the design in nature points to the Designer. By using reason and logic to interpret the order in the natural world, we can go beyond intelligent design and argue for God's existence. A fixed order must have a cause for that order, as Aquinas concludes: "By his natural reason man is able to arrive at some knowledge of God. For seeing that natural things run their course according to a fixed order, and since there cannot be order without a cause of order, men, for the most part, perceive that there is one who orders the things that we see" (Aquinas, 1905).

The Designer as God the Son

The above arguments for the existence of God generally apply to God the Father. But what about the second person of the Trinity, or God the Son? Specified complexity and DNA give evidence as a point of contact between the material and the infinite, with a designer as the most logical conclusion for the complex order in the universe. As such, Christ also makes for an interesting choice as the designer, the materially manifested member of the Trinity with a human ancestry (Rom. 9:5). If science is the process of going from the known to the unknown, the scientific evidence is highly consistent with the proposition found in Colossians 1:17: "He [Christ] is before all things, and in him all things hold together." Christ is the principle of cohesion in the universe and the Son, at this moment, is "sustaining all things by his powerful word" (Heb. 1:3).

For an age where "science is king," Christianity is the only "religion" where metaphysical beliefs were confirmed with inspection, rendering Christianity as the most realistic of any belief system. Every founder of an ideology or religion is dead in his grave. But the evidence for the resurrection is testable through the science of textual criticism. Overwhelming documentary attestation through the historical method corroborates the resurrection of Christ as the most substantiated event from antiquity. We don't have video evidence of the resurrection, but we don't need it. Called documentation and manuscript evidence, Scientists have validated that the historical method used at the time Scripture was written was very accurate. The existence of multiple independent eyewitness testimony, which was the best known forensic science of the day (and still is the primary form of evidence in criminal and civil law), affirm Christ as deity in the flesh. Enemy attestation of New Testament events, along with verifiable names and places anchored in historical records, betray the collusion and myth charge. That Jesus took on legendary status early does not mean myth in the fiction sense. Jesus became a legend in the sense we would use today when we say, "Michael Jordan is a legend in the game of basketball." He has taken on legendary status *based on the great things he did.* Events spurred the writings of the New Testament, not visa-versa.

Skepticism is not a modern phenomenon and the disciples, before engaging the culture, used their senses to empirically confirm His resurrection. They examined the nail scars in Christ's hands as well as the spear wound in His side (John 20:27). According to John, three of the five senses were used to validate the resurrected Christ: sight, sound, and touch (1 John 1:1-3) where the physical affirmed the metaphysical. The resurrection validated everything Jesus said and did in life which was reassessed, rethought, and related in the gospel accounts (John 2:22). Before Luke the physician "decided to write an orderly account," he "carefully investigated everything from the beginning" (Luke 1:39). And Paul the lawyer, trained in Hebrew education, categorized Christ's words and deeds into one of the greatest treatises in literature called the book of Romans. The basis of the Christian faith is the experiential affirmation of God penetrating time and space, which is not a blind faith but one based on observation, knowledge and reason. The claims of Christianity hung on the historical resurrection and great pains were taken to validate its occurrence. History is truth and Christ is the physical evidence a material world needs when testing for God. French mathematician, philosopher, and theologian Blaise Pascal said, "All who have claimed to know God and to prove his existence without Jesus Christ have done so ineffectively...Apart from him, and without Scripture...it is impossible to prove absolutely that God exists...But through and in Jesus Christ we can prove God's existence..." (Houston 1997, 147). Jesus "has made him known" (John. 1:18) and with Christ in the flesh, we can better conceive of and relate to God. Jesus is the entry point that unlocks the supernatural for people, the material/supernatural interface.

Information is a detectable arena where an intelligent source influences physical stuff. John 1:1 says, "in the beginning was the Word, and the Word was with God, and the Word was God." Jesus is the Word, or *logos* in the original Greek. *Logos* comes from the root word *lego*, meaning "to say" or "speak." John may have been realigning to Christ the aberrant Greek philosophy of stoicism, where one must get in line with the *logos* or "universal reason." But *logos* is information. And though the *Logos* is more than information, the Word becoming flesh is no less than information. If we do not observe God under a microscope or a designer moving particles, He could certainly be in the business of imparting information, the material/immaterial interface. This is one way of understanding how all things hold together in Him. Information exists in biology, the mystery of DNA, and the chemical language of A, C, T, and G where information is contemporaneous with, but not reduced to, physical processes.

The word *biology* also contains the root word *logos*, where "bios" means "life" and "logos" means "the knowledge of." Biology is literally "the study of life," a legitimate information/physical confluence. Information is the bridge from the immaterial to the material and points to a designer creating and influencing the physical world in complex and specified ways. Since design is found in nature, and nature in itself cannot account for its own design, it is logical to conclude that a designer shapes the arrangement through information. Information, *logos*, and the Word becoming flesh in Scripture are all related concepts. Because of the historical evidence, liberal scholars have conceded that Jesus was a real person who lived 2000 years ago. But a ludicrous question arises according to evolutionary logic: if Jesus' mother Mary evolved from chimps, is Jesus also subject to genetic relations with monkeys? Not if Mary was created in the image of God according to the information in Genesis 1:27.

The resurrection of Christ is the spiritual/material concursion and God's approval of His Son's perfect sacrifice for sin on the cross has empirical evidence. Though our culture overemphasizes the material, the resurrection shows that the material realm is not evil. God is spirit but the material realm, through "Christ's physical body" (Col. 1:22), has a crucial role in the redemption of all things. The reason Christ shared our humanity is because we "have flesh and blood," and "he had to be made like his brothers in every way" to "make atonement for the sins of the people" (Heb. 2:14,17). Eternal life incorporates the physical as believers will have endless, glorified physical experiences according to Romans 6:5: "if we have been united with him in a death like his, we will certainly also be united with him in a resurrection like his." Matter is not evil and the resurrection of Christ is not only committed materialists' *best* hope of preserving what is most important about this life into the next, the resurrection is their *only* hope. The design empirically verified in nature better helps us understand why the Bible says, "The wrath of God is being revealed from heaven against all the godlessness and wickedness of men who suppress the truth by their wickedness, since what may be known about God is plain to them, because God made it plain to them" (Rom. 1:18–19).

God Is Not at Odds with Science, He's Ahead of It

There has been an attempt to retain biblical credibility by saying that the Bible pertains to spiritual matters whereas science is the expert in the world of matter, as though the two areas are like parallel railroad tracks that never cross. It is an effort to "rescue" the Bible from its apparent lack of detail in scientific phenomena or its "primitive" mythical accounts of creation. However, to say God is not the definitive expert in the tangible realm goes against the evidence for God's existence as the source of creation. Such assertions neglect to consider that every writer of Scripture, in the 1500 years since Genesis was written, understood the book of Genesis as history. Genesis is foundational not only in understanding Scripture, but the physical world as well. The Bible does deliver an essential framework of creation events regarding the principle of life, and the six days of creation present abiogenesis. Some Scripture employs allegory and phenomenological language to depict absolute realities, but not Genesis.

Charles Darwin said, "On the ordinary view of each species having been independently created, we gain no scientific explanation." The "ordinary view" he is deriding is the account of the decisive and independent creation events of Genesis. But science does support the creation account, and creationism can be framed in a testable, five point, scientific model. Since Scripture preceded science, the biblical model of nature accommodates and predicts the evidences in scientific research and renders Christianity more than just a matter of faith. *The first tenet in the biblical model of science is that God created life in a sudden, optimal and fully functional capacity.* Genesis 1:20-24 report that at God's command, birds, fish, wild animals and livestock were produced. Complete adaptation packages, irreducible complexity, and the explosion of fully formed life forms in the fossil record refute Darwin's gradualism and affirm the abrupt appearance of life. One former evolutionist writes, "The lack of transitional forms in fossil and living entities is why evolutionists have the 'missing link' problem...The 'missing links'...will never be found because the Creator did not create transitional forms between kinds of creatures" (Martin 2008, 92-93).

The second tenet in the biblical model is that there is a biological separation of creatures as distinct species. Scientific naturalists can't even agree on how a species differs from a transition or a variation. Trying to prove transitional descent is not merely a problem of taxonomy but goes to the core of biology. The cells of birds and fish, for example, are different. The amino acids of amphibians, the supposed link from fish to land creatures, disqualify them as an intermediate form. Without molecular evidence for major taxonomical relationships, macroevolution is dead. However, Genesis 1:11, 20, and 25 perfectly explain the right balance in nature when they reveal that different species were created "according to their kinds." Though the "kinds" in Scripture are not species or genus per se, the biblical model of science is consistent with the general fixity and uniqueness of species observed in nature. Even Harvard biologist Gould acknowledged, "This notion of species as 'natural kinds'...fit splendidly with creationists tenets" (Gould 1979, 18). Early observations about an original design are often the most accurate, which is why Job's philosophy four thousand years ago incorporated verse 12 from chapter 11: "But a witless man can no more become wise than a wild donkey's colt can be born a man." Adaptation, where the Creator produced a standard gene set that could be modified through varying gene expressions, is not primary speciation and does violate Genesis chapter 1.

The third tenet in the biblical model of science is that God fashioned humans and animals to share physical characteristics from preexisting materials. Though creatures are essentially different, the Bible presents, and science confirms, how species share common blueprints of design in biochemistry, anatomy, physiology, and genetics. Genesis 2:19 says, "Now the Lord God had formed *out of the ground* all the wild animals and all the birds in the sky" (emphasis added). From His raw materials, the Creator fashioned analogous genetic building blocks for a broad spectrum of organisms that display similar design features. Unity does not mean ancestral descent from one living filament, rather, it is the use of like elements that creatures share such as oxygen, carbon, hydrogen etc. The biblical model of unity with distinction presents the exact combination of separation and resemblance that we observe among species. It all comes down to correct interpretation. Evolutionary developmental biologist Sean Carroll at the University of Wisconsin, Madison acknowledges that "The building blocks of squids and flies and humans and snakes are stunningly similar." Then he goes beyond science and interprets this as chance based "descent with modification" (Carroll, *Smithsonian* 47). A similar platform of materials is better explained through a biblical model of science where God fashioned animals to share physical characteristics from preexisting materials in an original design. A word about secondary causes. Evolutionists are obsessed with finding mechanisms, as though these would answer everything in biology. But the establishment of a mechanism says nothing about its origin. Everything can have a spiritual and an empirical explanation (which aren't mutually exclusive) and the Bible delivers a holistic explanation without disconnecting the physical from its spiritual cause. Limited by its domain, nomenclature and manifold appeal the uni-dimensional physical description, as emphasized in textbooks, only absorbs one part of our souls. An emphasis on mechanisms and secondary causes can also lead to a deistic position, where God set the creation ball rolling but is now removed. However, God directly creating physical mechanisms, through which some elements of creation were then generated by His fiat and command, are not at odds with creationism or His active providence. God formed nature, uses nature and actively commands nature for His purposes. Genesis 1:11 reports, "Then God said, 'Let the *land* produce vegetation: seed-bearing plants and trees on the land that bear fruit with seed in it...'" Genesis 2:6 reveals that "*streams* came up from the earth and watered the whole surface of the ground." God is in direct command of all force, matter, time, space, and energy; if His use of secondary mechanisms is mysterious, natural phenomena in science are not inconsistent with an infinite and personal God.

The fourth tenet in the biblical model of science is that Adam and Eve were the first humans created by God in the Middle East and possessed distinct features as creatures in His image. We derive this principle from several verses. Genesis 2:7 says, "the Lord God formed the man...", and Genesis 2:22 says, "Then God made a woman..." Putting these together with Genesis 2:15 identifies the location of the first humans in Iraq: "The Lord God took the man and put him in the Garden of Eden..." The Bible says man first inhabited the Garden of Eden, which some scholars say can refer to a broad region in the Middle East. Science is lining up with the biblical account of man's origin today more than ever. Scientists have now traced all genetic markers back to a single ancestral sequence and primordial pair known as *Y Chromosomal Adam* and *Mitochondrial Eve*.

Every male today can be traced back to a single man, and every woman is descended from one female. Also, the fact that humans lack genetic diversity indicates humans originated from a single location and small population, according to a fundamental law of genetics. Since Africans have the greatest genetic diversity, humanity must have originated near or in the Middle East or Africa. The origin of man sourced to a single location and small population somewhere near the Middle East has become known as the *Out of Africa* model. It contradicts the long held evolutionary *Multi-Regional Hypothesis*, where humans evolved from *homo erectus* by chance and convergence in multiple locations around Europe and Africa (Rana and Ross 2015).

The other element in this fourth tenet of the biblical model of science is that humans are unique from all other creatures as made in God's image. Genesis 1:26 says, "Let us make man in our image, in our likeness..." Being made in God's image means humans possess greater mental faculties than animals such as logic, reason, symbolic thought, complex language, moral discernment of right and wrong, creativity, and worship capacity (Rana and Ross 2015). Evolutionists like to categorize everything upright and bi-pedal as human. But archaeology continually vindicates that humans are not only distinct from animals but are also separate from the australopithecines and the so-called predecessors to humanity, which are just extinct animals. Genesis 2:7 states God directly created man from dust and became animated from His breath; man didn't evolve from primates or some preexisting pseudo human prototype. Science affirms the Biblical authority regarding the distinction of man. And the biblical model wrestles back science from atheistic gradualism and puts it back under a definitive theistic universe.

The fifth tenet in a biblical model of creation is that God created two distinct sexes as the primary means of procreation for species. Genesis 1:27 says "…male and female he created them." Reproduction is an incredibly complex phenomenon that Darwinists have a difficult time explaining from chance. But procreation is perfectly feasible as a product of design. If God created male and female from the beginning (Mark 10:6), it is impossible to fathom the molecule to man process over long ages. On a broader level, the world can be characterized in binary terms, whether male and female, light and darkness, creation and Creator, etc. One specialist reported that geniuses show the tendency to distinguish the superior from the inferior very early on in life and think in binary terms. Since the laws of thought are also the laws of things (Lewis 1967, 63), the ability to distinguish difference (whether good from evil or male from female) is a mark of intelligence through the timeless laws of logic. The bleeding of distinctions today, whether in gender blending, species merging, globalization (*One Human Family*), or national border disintegration are all influenced by evolutionary thought and an antinomian spirit against the principle of unity with distinction in creation. Political globalization, where man clumps to find safety in others, is a form of humanism that seeks the security of men over the security of God. The first attempt of globalization at Babel was thwarted by God, and he can do so again with our technological towers of Babel today.

Darwinism's Deadly Social Effects

Albert Einstein said, "Science without religion is lame; religion without science is blind." Science is only one means for knowledge and is not the highest. The absolutes of what God said in His Word are the destinations of all scientific inquiry, if science even gets there. The sufficiency of Scripture is outstanding when stacked against its competitor in the origin of life scenario. Evolution's fallacy of composition means we are merely subordinated to the value of materials in the physical realm. That is, humans consist only of stardust and sink to the status of amoral animals descended from chimps. The net effect cheapens life and subsidizes policies of death such as abortion, euthanasia and eugenics. Even a world war, where millions of people were killed, was based on closed system naturalism. When Jews were told they were nothing but "soil and blood," Nazi Germany assumed racial superiority by applying the principles of natural selection and evolution to humans. If nature's breeder keeps populations in check, atheistic dictators usurp the same role to control populations through mass slaughters and holocausts. (There's no greater symbol of relativism than tyranny). World War II reveals that science, devoid of ethics, can still lead to unintellectual barbarism. And broader history shows that when Christians are extirpated from a society, culture becomes oppressive. The contrasting worldviews are illustrated by quotes from their respective sources. Charles Darwin wrote, "A scientific man ought to have no wishes, no affections— a mere heart of stone." Hearts of stone lead to cultures of death. God says, "I will give you a new heart and put a new spirit in you; I will remove from you your heart of stone and give you a heart of flesh" (Ez. 36:26). If Darwin is still in the grave, it might be better to trust God's assessment.

People as nothing more than overgrown blobs of biology, or a random collision of molecules from some chemical ocean, has contributed to all kinds of existential and psychological delusions about reality. One researcher argues that codependent relationships are sourced in closed system thinking, where people try to extract all of their satisfaction and meaning out of others. Morally passive child-rearing, by parents who have absolved any sense of right and wrong, can be traced to closed system beliefs and the amorality of man. Political positions favoring abortion are based on a fear of over-population because of closed system naturalism. (It's okay for an abortionist to be on the planet or as Ronald Reagan put it, "I've noticed that 100% of those who are for abortion have been born"). Opposed to the mystery of God's ways, those who rely on big government as the cure to all human ills assume a world under sealed material determinism. "Man is destined to be governed by God or by tyrants," said William Penn and closed system secularism facilitates the slide to despotism. Anxiety over the planet's destruction, through man caused climate change, is rooted in humanism, an over-exalted view of man and closed system reasoning. (Leading environmental authority Dr. Fred Singer says that "human activities are _not_ influencing the global climate in perceptible ways", and Genesis 8:22 reveals that "as long as the earth endures…cold and heat…will never cease," —Martin 2008, 306, 312). The deadly nature of atheistic evolution as a social construct is revealed by what mass murderer Jeffrey Dahmer said after he killed 17 men: "I had believed the lie that we came from the slime. I reasoned that what's the point of trying to modify my behavior if there is no judgment, or a Creator to be accountable to?" (Dahmer 1994). Atheistic evolution leads to all kinds of pathologies and, in a closed system, we fight and sue for everything we can because this world is all there is.

On the other hand, the Bible elevates the dignity of man as made in God's image. Life is valuable endemically and not just when a utilitarian purpose is discerned. Scripture affirms a moral law in the hearts of all men and is the basis of human rights ethics around the world. If natural man was true to his Darwinian philosophy, he shouldn't rescue animals and treat sick people with a "weak constitution," to use Darwin's term. When naturalists heal the weak, they contradict their own principle which says to "let the strongest live and the weakest die" (Darwin 1859). It is the Bible that verifies an innate sense of right and wrong hardwired into all men and reveals our altruism. Scripture explains our world perfectly when it says we are created for transcendent significance and what we are now experiencing is a depraved nature in a paradise lost. This worldview is most consistent with, and a return to, reality. If detailed scientific phenomenon, such as exists in a quantum mechanics textbook, was our greatest need it would be in the Bible. Since it is not in the Bible, it is not our greatest need. As one man observed:

> Western culture rejected the mystery and transcendence of the Middle Ages and placed its confidence in pragmatism and progress, the pillars of the Modern Era. But once we rid ourselves of the Author, it didn't take long to lose the larger story (Eldredge 2001).

Is Matter All That Matters to You?

"Anyone who comes to him," says Hebrews 11:6, "must believe that he exists." Someone may ask, "What if God doesn't exist? Isn't the existence of God an argument from silence either way?" Not if God is not silent, and there is plenty of evidence if one wants to peer into it. "There can be no demonstration of God except through some effect of His production," writes Aquinas, "because the principle of demonstration is a definition of the thing defined" (Aquinas

1905, Book 1, XXV,52). With the existence of God, it's a small step to accept miracles, the supernatural, cataclysmic events, and the resurrection. One apologist says, "If the New Testament documents are historical, then the miracles are actual." Even from an historical position, Scripture is its own authority and contains the most accurate and complete words pertaining to the supernatural realm. Romans chapter 1 says all men "knew God" (1:21). But when they "did not think it worthwhile to retain the knowledge of God, he gave them over to a depraved mind" (1:28) and "their thinking became futile" (1:21). Atheistic Darwinism is one offshoot of futile thinking where people willfully disbelieve the internal and external evidence for the knowledge of God.

Naturalists must answer the questions as to whether this world is normal and belief in God weird? Or is there something deeply and fundamentally wrong with this world and God is a return to reality? Though some spiritual truths seem illogical, we are built for reason and have used logic, science and evidence to argue for the existence of God. To be sure, there are other ways of knowing things other than the empirical method. (Socrates said that virtues were sources of knowledge and Paul prayed people might know the "love [of God] that surpasses knowledge" Eph. 3:19). But science supports the existence of a Designer and the most accurate assessment of the metaphysical realm is found in Scripture. We may acknowledge the existence of God, but how to know Him personally is the issue. The Bible tells us everything we need to know about God, how to know Him and live forever. One music icon said, "death is what you leave behind you, it's not so much where you're going." But if eternity is real, it does matter where you are going; the stakes are high and this life is but a dot on the line of perpetuity. Scripture pronounces sin as the greatest of human problems, causing not only separation and death from Him but misinterpretations about Him. Attributing the design found in nature to chance, with no spiritual realities, is a distortion sourced in creaturely separation and deprivation.

Despite sin's corrupting effect on man's ability to interpret life correctly, God reveals Himself in nature and all men innately know on some level that God exists. Psalm 19:1 says "the skies proclaim the works of his hands" and people are without excuse about some knowledge of God. An innate knowledge of God doesn't mean an intimate knowledge of Him because people suppress the truth (Rom. 1:18) and are born with a nature that opposes the Spirit of God (Gal. 5:17). Natural man needs to do nothing to remain in spiritual error and his "earthly nature" (Col. 3:5) must be put to death for new life to sprout. Even natural people who study nature and science have a corrupted disposition that can cause strange interpretations about reality. It may offend naturalists (who believe that everything natural must be right) to say their sin nature must spiritually die with Christ in order to live. When Chesterton was asked what he thought the greatest problem in the world was, he replied, "I am." Or as Tolstoy put it, "Everybody thinks of changing the world. No one thinks of changing himself." The greatest predicament is not oil prices, international tensions or the economy but man and his natural nature out of alignment with God. Only the Bible reveals the marvelous antidote of God coming in the flesh to die for our earthly nature and be reconciled to the God and Father of our souls. Laying our sin at the cross of Christ is the only way of truly changing ourselves and the world.

If a heavy minded highbrow has a quibble with the design argument, he or she is missing the trees for the forest. As the god of the world system against God, Satan is brilliant and will always supply some counterfeit system of thought people can latch onto if they don't want God or a change of heart. Apparent consistency or coherence within a thought system like evolution does not necessarily mean that arrangement corresponds to reality. If Satan can't prevent one from believing in God, he will try to thwart an accurate view of Him. Not only is the Christian worldview logical, but any other is deceitful. One does not commit intellectual suicide in coming to Christ and Christian truth is the highest in thought. Faith is required in any origin of life theory, but the preponderance of evidence points to design. (Faith in the secular sense is hoping for something to be true; faith in the biblical sense is present trust in a future reality). As a purposeless and chance laden molecules to man process, atheistic evolution requires more faith than believing in creation by God. For those unwilling to be morally accountable to God, which is the real motive behind atheistic naturalism, more reasons merely supply additional fuel for misinterpretation. At some point, one must make a conscious decision for Christ and there is enough evidence to make an informed decision regarding your eternal destiny.

Evidence for the Christian God is overwhelming. We are designed to worship and know Him, and we can only operate at full capacity in Him. The infinite God is capable of being known intimately in relationship by anyone. The Apostle Paul said, "all things were created by him and for him" (Col. 1:16). Pascal put it in scientific terms, "there is a God shaped vacuum in the human heart only He was meant to fill." And the Westminster Shorter Catechism summarized the purpose of life in delightful terms: "The chief end of man is to glorify God and enjoy him forever." Pleasure, enjoyment and service in Him are the end game, and Christianity is the only "religion" that is not really a religion but a relationship with God. To configure a whole system of politics or science without God and think we are happier and better off is delusional. If existence is attributed to a gracious God, how is God harmful when woven into scientific theory? At some point, you must make a conscious decision for Christ and there is a juncture when more reasons and external proofs won't help. Knowing God is ultimately a heart issue, an act of the will, and an inside job cultivated by reading His word. We may "accept man's testimony, but God's testimony is greater" (1 John 5: 9).

There is more to life than this world and the position one takes with the Creator has eternal consequences one way or the other. As C.S. Lewis put it, "Aim at heaven and you get this world thrown in. Aim at earth and you get neither." Those who do not trust Christ in this life will live in eternal separation and punishment as 2 Thessalonians 1:8 indicates: "He will punish those who do not know God or obey the gospel of the Lord Jesus." Scripture reveals that man's sin nature and natural enemyship keeps a man shaking an inward fist at God. Though not politically correct to talk about, there is a part in us that knows John Calvin is right when he said, "the wrath of God lies upon all men so long as they continue sinners" (Calvin 2008, 490). Law descends from God and a law Darwin didn't consider is the law of blood. The law of blood says that something must die for something else to live. Transgression requires blood for iniquity which helps explain the impulse we have to punish those who wrong us. But any mortal's blood will not remove our separation and fatal hostility towards God. (Natural man's solution of exacting the blood of another mortal in rage and revenge is a counterfeit to Christ's work). A radical problem requires a radical solution and only sinless deity in the flesh, as a one-time sacrifice, can satisfy God's wrath against our sin and solve man's sin problem for all time (Heb. 10:10).

Suffering precedes honor in many endeavors on earth and no less is true regarding the salvation of our souls. Since we are spiritual *and* physical creatures, a personal member of the triune deity took on flesh to shed His holy blood as compensation for the blood requirement of offences. God's wrath against our violation was poured out on His Son once for all time, which allows those who trust in Him to forgive others. He is an expert at the greatest plague of mankind, and He is fully capable when He took care of our sin. The blood of Christ not only removed our separation from God but allowed us to be credited with His blamelessness and be set free to live in Him. Each person has an individual day in court at the judgment seat of Christ and one must believe in Christ before death as the antidote to the guilt of sin to live forever. The time for then is now; after death is too late. If a person responds to the design testimony of God in nature, God will see to it that more precise biblical truth will be found so a decision for Christ can be made.

There is an interesting correlation between those that believe empiricism (the senses) is the height of knowledge and those who live a life of sensual indulgence. If sin can be horrifying to admit and the condemnation of violating moral law burdening, we might latch onto any impotent system of thought, like scientific atheism, to rationalize it away. At its root, Darwinism is an attack against the truth of God and His universe, showing that hostility and rebellion can still be presented in intellectual and professional terms. Design confronts humanists that they are not on the thrones of their lives and any hint of a moral realm implied by the design in nature is fiercely resisted by naturalists; the spiritual domain means moral accountability and judgment for sin, which many would rather not give up. Yet, the scientific atheist who does not acknowledge God's design has a small and limited mind; intelligence without God's Spirit and moral development is still evil. Christianity is logical, comprehensive, cohesive and exhaustive in articulating the issues of life even as it is anchored in history and science; the world makes sense through the big picture of a biblical lens. The design in nature, as well as evidence of corruption within it, are accurate to the biblical notions of a beautiful God-created universe that is also subject to a curse. Naturalistic psychologists and anthropologists will never understand the world or human nature without a biblical view of man, who is made in God's image yet depraved in nature. Darkness and night are realities that science will never fully master or articulate (John 1:4). A curse placed on the earth, as Genesis 3:17 describes, is the best explanation as to why creation has problems and Christianity is the most accurate, relevant and realistic worldview. The intellect is involved, but knowing Christ is a heart issue. If people "are darkened in their understanding and separated from the life of God [it is] because of the ignorance that is in them due to the hardening of their hearts" (Eph. 4:18).

Like Jesus' disciples who were amazed that "Even the winds and the waves obey him" (Matt. 8:27), we are all recovering naturalists when we discover how God is working in an apparent random world of secondary causes. Some profess to know God, but when it comes down to obeying Him in the trenches of life are practical atheists.

If a skeptic is more convinced that God exists after reading this study, it is important to distinguish a belief *that* God exists from a personal belief *in* God. A greater inclination to affirm *the* savior after this study doesn't mean He is *your* savior. You have to make Him personal by choice. Don't buy the lie that living without Christ escapes suffering because Scripture says, "the way of the transgressor is hard" (Prov. 13:15 KJV). Won't you put your trust in Christ today and begin experiencing peace, rest, purpose, forgiveness, grace and life forever? If you have never done so, your time is now. It's not in becoming religious, performing good works or cleaning your life up; just believe and trust. Proofs and evidence in this book can assist us to believe verses like Romans 10:9: "If you declare with your mouth, 'Jesus is Lord,' and believe in your heart that God raised him from the dead, you will be saved." His kingdom is the only thing that will last forever and that future will arrive. Let God take care of the fears, consequences or stigmas you may have in coming to Him. When you trust in Christ, get into a good Bible teaching church and begin the journey of obeying His ways. The Bible is a source of information and propositional truth man does not reason to on his own, and further answers to lingering questions will be internally verified. The "full riches of complete understanding" happens in community where hearts are "united in love" (Col. 2:2).

AFTERWORD

⸺⸻⸺

ENGAGING THE CULTURE IS A mandate for the believer in Christ. Scripture allocates for periods of reformation, preparation, and self-examination. But Christianity also looks outward and initiates with society. Assertion without equipment can be a prescription for failure and the arguments for intelligent design are a powerful instrument in the toolbox of the believer to reach a sophisticated culture. How do we bridge the gap between this world and the next for a culture given over to Darwinian naturalism as the best explanation for life? By unpacking the layers and destroying the strongholds of evolution that are "raised up against the knowledge of God" (2 Cor. 10:4–5).

God has allowed great systems of thought to be built up against His truth. With the rise of homeschooling and Christian colleges, Christians in the last century have tended toward disengaging from those so called "worldly complicated theories of science," as much out of mental laziness as for any spiritual reasons. The inability to refute evolution has left doubt in the minds of many believers about the veracity of creationism or even the Bible, due to the intricate volumes about life as a product of natural causes. The folds of Darwinian evolution are layered, harboring lies, deceptions, and the "wickedness of men who suppress the truth" (Rom. 1:18). And the concepts in evolution are important to grasp so that we may be "prepared to give an answer and reason for the hope within us" (1 Pet. 3:15). Darwinism is an extensive arena in which to "correctly handle the word of truth" (2 Tim. 2:15) so that men may repent "for a knowledge of the truth" (2 Tim. 2:25). Getting knowledge and becoming equipped for this kind of apologetic is never an inconsequential use of time, since God has a way of using everything we have learned for His kingdom's sake. As the world is deep, so Christians should be deeper.

This guide has exposed the fatal errors of evolutionary biology and fills in residual cracks of skepticism about origins, "supply[ing] what is lacking in your faith" (1 Thes. 3:10). Apologetics is not just for unbelievers. It is also for Christ followers who can then refute worldly theories with less fear, when their own uncertainties have been addressed. At minimum, believers should be familiar with the notions that mold our modern world and study what comprises our intellectual culture, much like Daniel was schooled in the highest learning of Babylon before God's Word took preeminence. Apologetics can take a variety of forms, and the discordant philosophies of the world (of which evolutionary biology is a major component) deserve to be confronted in their own right. As C. S. Lewis said, "Good philosophy must exist, if for no other reason, because bad philosophy needs to be answered" (Lewis 1980, 28).

This manual is also designed to transcend denominations and systems of thought within evangelical circles, including the wall between old-earth and young-earth creationists. Both branches of creationism hold the Genesis account of origins as historical and literal on some level. But old-earth creationists feel certain uses of the Hebrew word "yom" (day) can allow for a day in the six days of creation as a long age, accommodating research from many areas of science for an old universe. Old earthers ask whether God is deceiving us with the instruments and the amount of data affirming deep time, or whether long age is necessarily at odds with a deep God. When the scientific data (with some assumptions) pointing to deep time is juxtaposed with Scripture, some novel interpretive positions result that one might not arrive at from a plain reading. For example, some old earth creationists believe there was a long gap after the "Spirit of God was hovering over the waters" (Gen. 1:2) but before the days of creation. Also, if a day of creation could be a long age, then animal death of the fossil record occurred before Adam fell (Adam was the last to be created on day six and land animals were created early on day six, with birds/fish created on day five).

Even though the Bible says God formed man from the dust, old earthers say this could mean that God animated Adam from a pre-existing, proto-human upright form and breathed His image bearing qualities into him on the sixth day. If elements of this hermeneutic are innovative, old earthers have contributed deep insights from the world of biology to refute evolution that have been considered in this book.

Young earthers say the old earth position is the scientific tail wagging the theological dog. As its own authority, Scripture shouldn't be viewed through a scientific lens as the starting point, which results in a creation account nestling too closely with evolutionary assumptions. Young earth creationists would ask if God is deceiving us with the plain sense of the word "day" in Genesis since the Hebrew word for "yom," when accompanied with a number, always refers to a literal 24-hour period in Genesis. Centering on the genealogies as generally complete historical records, they say there is no such thing as an old earth position and the earth is young at 6,200 years old (some young earthers believe the earth is 25,000 to 100,000 years old). Because age of the earth interpretation extends beyond just the age of the earth, young earthers point out that an old earth is sourced in faulty assumptions that lead to incorrect conclusions in other areas. For example, an old earth necessitates animal death before the fall which affects doctrines like sin, death and the gospel itself. A plain reading of Genesis through the New Testament connotes instant, cataclysmic and system-wide death beginning when Adam and Eve sinned in the garden of Eden in Genesis chapter 3, and which Christ's death began to eliminate. Young earthers would also ask how animal death is good when God saw his handiwork as "good" after each day of creation? According to many young earthers, if the simple gospel can be presented clearly by both a young or old creationist, logical destinations stemming from old earth positions may, ironically, lead to subtle erosions that undermine the gospel itself. From the law of noncontradiction, both creation accounts cannot be right. And young earthers would ask what is wrong with a tight and literal interpretation of the Genesis text that coheres with the rest of Scripture and has scientific credibility?

All believers agree that faith in Jesus is not enough if the literal account of origins in Scripture is abrogated. A distrust in the plain, historical Hebrew relation of Genesis threatens the meaning of sin, a literal Adam and Eve, the cross, and the gospel itself. If these are spurious, what confidence do we have in the resurrection? One apologist challenges:

> Is it possible that we have been seduced by the world's 'convincing arguments of academia,' impressive credentials and the ensuing 'success, power, and prominence' that comes from finding truth apart from God's Word?...Many young people

in churches and Christian schools are on the broad road that leads to destruction...due in large part to wishy-washy teaching about the Creation, and ultimately, the Creator (Martin 2008, 274, 318).

Though old-earth creationists have embraced the design movement more so than young-earth creationists, both sides can utilize the arguments in this guide to understand the framework of evolutionary thought and refute its premises on its own terms. It is possible to use long age concepts for the purposes of refuting theories woven into them. Apprehending the concepts and nomenclature of Darwinism, to expose its fallacies, does not have to abrogate a young earth position. Some Christians believe that presenting reasons for design, along with apologetics in general, are needless middle steps in evangelizing others. They "reason" that the use of logical proofs holds little value.

No clear-thinking believer disagrees with the sufficiency of Scripture or the role of the Holy Spirit in engaging others. We are built for logic and the faith we observe is a reasonable one with much evidence. Or as Aquinas said, "sin cannot entirely take away from man the fact that he is a rational being" (Aquinas, 1905 Book 1). All final truth is God's truth (as truth by its nature must be), and a defense of the faith can extend to many levels in "proving from the Scriptures that Jesus was the

Christ" (Acts 18:28). The God given rational thought override to our instinctual base nature is part of what it means to be human and made in God's image. As Matthew Henry put it, "the Gospel supports the rule of right reason and conscience over appetite and passion." There are many ways of knowing things, and logic is endemic to how we think, the basis of attitudes, emotions and lifestyle. Depending on the Lord and trusting the Holy Spirit are not at odds with the work of being equipped to give an answer for the hope within us (1 Pet. 3:15). A sophisticated society often requests evidence to back truth claims, including the correct interpretation of evidence using the scientific method. Even if their theological positions are unclear, the evidences for design uncovered by researchers can be part of a bigger process of loosening deeply rooted Darwinian thought in *preevangelising* those enslaved by closed system naturalism. Predestination notwithstanding, how do we reply to an atheist who asserts that evolution is the principle of life? How do we answer someone who asks us why we believe God exists?

The intent of this series is not to make arrogant with knowledge (1 Cor. 8:1) or to win an argument. The aim is to look for entry points to defend the faith in conversations that arise about evolution, origins or even the gospel. One does not need to be a scholar or scientist to engage others; one just needs a working knowledge of the issues at hand in the theory. This guide will even supply strong arguments to elite scientists who may know more than we do. But most people we encounter will only have a basic familiarity with evolution. We do not have to know everything in order to say something and establish credibility at "the water cooler" as informed believers. The purpose of our apologetic is to point people to Christ, the source of all truth, and use any opening to talk about the greater truths of Christianity.

BIBLICAL VERSES WITH APPLICATION TO APOLOGETICS

———◦◦◦———

the wisdom of the wise will perish, the intelligence of the intelligent will vanish

—Isaiah 29:14

Shall what is formed say to the one who formed it, "You did not make me"? Can the pot say to the potter, "You know nothing"?

—Isaiah 29:16

"Present your case," says the Lord. "Set forth your arguments," says Jacob's King.

—Isaiah 41:21

I am the Lord, the Maker of all things, who stretches out the heavens, who spreads out the earth by myself...who overthrows the learning of the wise and turns it into nonsense,

—Isaiah 44:24-25

You have trusted in your wickedness and have said, 'No one sees me.' Your wisdom and knowledge mislead you when you say to yourself, 'I am, and there is none besides me.'

—Isaiah 47:10

With this in mind, since I myself have carefully investigated everything from the beginning, I too decided to write an orderly account for you,

—Luke 1:39(a)

After his suffering, he presented himself to them and gave many convincing proofs that he was alive.

—Acts 1:3(a)

He [Saul] talked and debated with the Grecian Jews...

—Acts 9:29

The proconsul, an intelligent man, sent for Barnabas and Saul because he wanted to hear the word of God.

—Acts 13:7

As was his custom, Paul went into the synagogue, and on three Sabbath days he reasoned with them from the Scriptures, explaining and proving that the Messiah had to suffer and rise from the dead. "This Jesus I am proclaiming to you is the Messiah," he said.

—Acts 17:2-3

While Paul was waiting for them in Athens...So he reasoned in the synagogue with both Jews and God-fearing Greeks...

—Acts 17:16(a), 17(a)

Every Sabbath he [Paul] reasoned in the synagogue, trying to persuade Jews and Greeks.

—Acts 18:4

For he [Apolllos] vigorously refuted the Jews in public debate, proving from the Scriptures that Jesus was the Christ.

—Acts 18:28

Paul entered the synagogue and spoke boldly there for three months, arguing persuasively about the kingdom of God.

—Acts 19:8

[Paul] had discussions daily in the lecture hall of Tyrannus.

—Acts 19:9

"I am not insane, most excellent Festus," Paul replied. 'What I am saying is true and reasonable."

—Acts 26:25

We do, however, speak a message of wisdom among the mature, but not the wisdom of this age or of the rulers of this age, who are coming to nothing.

—1 Corinthians 2:6

"The Lord knows that the thoughts of the wise are futile."

—1 Corinthians 3:20

But knowledge puffs up while love builds up. Those who think they know something do not yet know as they ought to know.

—1 Corinthians 8:1-2

After [he was raised], he appeared to more than five hundred of the brothers and sisters at the same time...

—1 Corinthians 15:6

Be on your guard; stand firm in the faith; be courageous; be strong.

—1 Corinthians 16:13

so that you can answer those who take pride in what is seen rather than in what is in the heart.

—2 Corinthians 5:12(c)

We demolish arguments and every pretension that sets itself up against the knowledge of God, and we take captive every thought to make it obedient to Christ.

—2 Corinthians 10:5

Then we will no longer be infants, tossed back and forth by the waves, and blown here and there by every wind of doctrine and by the cunning and craftiness of men in their deceitful scheming.

—Ephesians 4:14

I tell you this so that no one may deceive you by fine-sounding arguments.

—Colossians 2:4

See to it that no one takes you captive through hollow and deceptive philosophy, which depends on human tradition and the basic principles of this world rather than on Christ.

—Colossians 2:8

Such a person goes into great detail about what he has seen, and his unspiritual mind puffs him up with idle notions.

—Colossians 2:18

so that you may know how to answer everyone.

—Colossians 4:6

For the appeal we make does not spring from error or impure motives, nor are we trying to trick you.

—1 Thessalonians 2:3

For this reason God sends them a powerful delusion so that they will believe the lie.

—2 Thessalonians 2:11

If anyone teaches false doctrines and does not agree to the sound instruction of our Lord Jesus Christ and to godly teaching, he is conceited and understands nothing...

—1 Timothy 6:3,4

Turn away from godless chatter and the opposing ideas of what is falsely called knowledge,

—1 Timothy 6:20(b)

Instead, to suit their own desires, they will gather around them a great number of teachers to say what their itching ears want to hear. They will turn their ears away from the truth...

—2 Timothy 4:3-4

so that he can encourage others by sound doctrine and refute those who oppose it.

—Titus 1:9(b)

This salvation, which was first announced by the Lord, was confirmed to us by those who heard him.

—Hebrews 2:3

Remember those earlier days, after you had received the light, when you stood your ground in a great contest in the face of suffering.

—Hebrews 10:32

Do not be carried away by all kinds of strange teachings.

—Hebrews 13:9

May the God of peace...equip you for every good thing for doing his will...

—Hebrews 13:20(a), 21

But in your hearts set apart Christ as Lord. Always be prepared to give an answer to everyone who asks you to give the reason for the hope that you have.

—1 Peter 3:15

I felt compelled to write and urge you to contend for the faith…

—Jude 1:3

Many deceivers, who do not acknowledge Jesus Christ as coming in the flesh, have gone out into the world…Watch out that you do not lose what you have worked for…

—2 John 1:7(a),8(a)

BIBLIOGRAPHY

Aquinas, Thomas. 1905. *Summa Contra Gentiles.* Translated by Joseph Rickaby. London: Burns and Oates.

Aquinas, Thomas. 1905. *Summa Contra Gentiles,* Book 1, Chapter XXV. Translated by Joseph Rickaby. London: Burns and Oates. Accessed November 2016. http:// catholicprimer.org/aquinas/aquinas_summa_contra_ gentiles.pdf.

Aquinas Thomas. *Summa Theologiae.* 1948. First Part. *Treatise on the One God. Question 2. The Existence of God.* Translated by the Fathers of the English Dominican Province. New York, NY: Benzinger Bros. Accessed November, 2016. www.sacred-texts.com/chr/aquinas/ summa/sum005.htm.

Atkins, Peter. 1995. *The Limitless Power of Science* in Nature's Imagination. John Cornwell, ed. Oxford UK: Oxford University Press.

Bapteste, Eric. January 21, 2009. Quoted in Graham Lawton. "Why Darwin was wrong about the tree of life," *New Scientist.*

Behe, Michael J. 1996. *Darwin's Black Box: The Biochemical Challenge to Evolution.* New York: Free Press.

Berg, Howard. Web References, Zoominfo.com. http://www.zoominfo.com/p/Howard- Berg/4307055. Accessed March 2017.

Brown, Walt. 2008. *In The Beginning: Compelling Evidence for Creation and the Flood.* Phoenix, AZ: Center for Scientific Creation.

Calvin, John. 1974. *Calvin's Commentaries, 22 Volume Set.* Grand Rapids, MI: Baker Books.

Calvin, John. 2008. *Institutes of the Christian Religion.* Translated by Henry Beveridge. Peabody, MA: Hendrickson Publishers, Inc.

Carroll, Sean. February 2009. *What Darwin Didn't Know. Today's Scientists Marvel that the 19th Century Naturalist's Grand Vision of Evolution is Still the Key to Life.* www.smithsonianmag.com/science-nature/what-darwin-didnt-know-45637001. Accessed December, 2017.

Chesterton, G.K. April 26, 1924. *Illustrated London News.* Quoted in www.morec.com/-schall/chestert.htm by James V. Schall. Accessed January, 2017.

Chesterton, G.K. 2009. *Orthodoxy.* Chicago, IL: Moody Publishers.

Chesterton, G.K. 1991. *The Collected Works of G. K. Chesterton: Volume XXXV:* The Illustrated London News: *1929-1931.* Edited by Lawrence J. Clipper; general editors: George J. Marlin, Richard P. Rabatin, and John L. Swan. San Francisco, CA: Ignatius Press.

Coyne, Jerry. 2007. *Don't Know Much Biology.* Accessed November, 2016. www.edge.org/conversation/don-39t-know-much-biology.

Cram, Donald J. 1990. *From Design to Discovery. Profiles, Pathways, and Dreams.* Washington DC: American Chemical Society.

Crichton, Michael. January 17, 2003. *Speech: Aliens Cause Global Warming.* California Institute of Technology. http://creation.com/crichton-on-scientific-consensus. Accessed March 2017.

Dahmer, Jeffrey and Stone Phillips. 1994. *Jeffrey Dahmer Interview by Stone Phillips*, Dateline NBC. Accessed November 2016. https://archive.org/details/Dahmer_on_Dateline_NBC.

Darwin, Charles. 1837. *Notebook B*. Accessed November, 2016. www.age-of-the-sage.org/evolution/charles_darwin/tree-of-life-sketch_1837.html.

Darwin, Charles. 1859. *On The Origin of Species by Means of Natural Selection, or The Preservation of Favoured Races in the Struggle for Life*. Accessed November, 2016. www.talkorigins.org/faqs/origin.html.

Darwin, Charles. 1872. *The Origin of Species by Means of Natural Selection, or The Preservation of Favoured Races in the Struggle for Life*. Sixth Edition. Accessed November, 2016. http://literature.org/authors/darwin-charles/the-origin-of-species-6th-edition/

Darwin, Charles. 1887. *The Autobiography of Charles Darwin*. The Unofficial Steven J. Gould Archive. www.stephenjaygould.org/library/darwin_autobiography. html. 1992.

Darwin, Charles. 1964. *The Origin of Species: A Facsimile of the First Edition*. Cambridge, MA: Harvard University Press.

Darwin, Charles. 1971. *The Origin of Species*, J.M. Dent & Sons Ltd, London.

Darwin, Charles. 2011. *On the Origin of Species.* Greensboro, NC: Empire Books.

Darwin, Erasmus. 1818. [Originally published 1794]. *Zoonomia; or the Laws of Organic Life.* 1 (4nd American ed.). Philadelphia, PA: Edward Earle.

Davis, Percival and Dean H. Kenyon. 1989. *Of Pandas and People: The Central Question of Biological Origins.* Dallas, TX: Houghton Publishing Co.

Davies, Paul. 1999. *The Fifth Miracle. The Search for the Origin and Meaning of Life.* New York, NY: Touchstone.

Dawkins, Richard. 2004. PBS Special with Bill Moyers, *Evolution Then and Now.* NOW. http://www.pbs.org/now/transcript/transcript349_full.html. Accessed March 2017.

Dawkins, Richard. November 30, 2013. *Q&A: Richard Dawkins discusses evolution, religion and his fans.* Los Angeles Times. http://articles.latimes.com/2013/nov-/30/science/la-sci-richard-dawkins-20131130#axzz2m TiaNF8V. Accessed March, 2017.

Dawkins, Richard. 2014. The Edge.Org. *What Scientific Idea is Ready for Retirement?* Accessed November 2016. www.edge.org/response-detail/25366.

Dawkins, Richard. 1986. *The Blind Watchmaker: Why the Evidence for Evolution Reveals a Universe Without Design.* New York, NY: W.W. Norton and Co.

Dawkins, Richard. April 15, 1982. "The Necessity of Darwinism." *New Scientist,* Vol. 94.

Dembski, William A. 2004. *The Design Revolution: Answering the Toughest Questions about Intelligent Design.* Nottingham: InterVarsity Press.

Dembski, William A., and Jonathan Wells. 2008. *The Design of Life: Discovering Signs of Intelligence in Biological Systems.* Dallas: Foundation for Thought and Ethics.

Dembski, William A., and Sean McDowell. 2008. *Understanding Intelligent Design: Everything You Need To Know in Plain Language.* Eugene, OR: Harvest House.

Denton, Michael. 1986. *Evolution: A Theory in Crisis.* Chevy Chase, MD: Adler & Adler Publishers, Inc.

Eldredge, John. 2001. *Wild at Heart. Discovering the Secrets of a Man's Soul.* Nashville: Thomas Nelson Publishers.

Evolution News and Views. Accessed March 20, 2013. www.evolutionnews.org/2012/11/oparin_he_got_i30 66681.html.

Geisler, Norman, and Ronald Brooks. 1990. *When Skeptics Ask, A Handbook O Christian Evidences*. Grand Rapids, MI: Baker Books.

Geisler, Norman, and Frank Turek. 2004. *I Don't Have Enough Faith to Be an Atheist*. Wheaton, IL: Crossway Books.

Gould, Stephen J. May 1977. "Evolution's Erratic Pace." *Natural History*. Vol. LXXXVI, No. 5.

Gould, Stephen J. August-September 1979. "A Quahog is a Quahog." *Natural History*. Vol. 88, No. 7.

Gould, Stephen J. 1980. *The Pandas Thumb*. New York, NY: W.W. Norton and Co. Inc.

Gould, Stephen J. February 1993. "Cordelia's Dilemma," *Natural History*.

Grasse, Pierre Paul. 1977. *Evolution of Living Organisms*. Cambridge, MA: Academic Press.

Graziano, Michael. 2013. *How the Light Gets Out. Consciousness is the 'Hard Problem' the One That Confounds and Philosophy. Has a New Theory Cracked it?* Accessed December 2016. https://aeon.co/essays/how-consciousness-works-and-why-we-believe-in-ghosts.

Goodall, Jane. November 27, 2009. *Bill Moyers Journal* transcript. Accessed December 2016. www.pbs.org/moyers/journal/11272009/transcript1.html.

Haldane, J.B.S. 2001. *Possible Worlds.* Hendron, VA: Transaction Publishers.

Harold, Franklin M. 2001. *The Way of the Cell: Molecules, Organisms and the Order of Life.* Oxford UK: Oxford University Press.

Hayden, Thomas. February 2009. *What Darwin Didn't Know.* Smithsonian Magazine. www.smithsonianmag.com/science-nature/what-darwin-didnt-know-45637001. Accessed December, 2017.

Houston, James. 1997. *Mind on First: A Faith for the Skeptical and Indifferent.* Minneapolis, MN: Bethany House Publishers.

Hawking, Stephen. September 10, 2010. *CNN Larry King Live* Broadcast.

Lawrence, D.H. 2012. *A Certain Difficult Repentance.* Accessed November, 2016. https://poetrytherapynews. com/2012/11/15/a-certain-difficult-repentance/

Lederman, Leon. With Dick Teresi. 2006. *The God Particle: If the Universe is the Answer, What is the Question?* New York, NY: Mariner Books.

Lewis, C.S. 2001. *Mere Christianity.* Harper San Francisco, CA: Zondervan Publishing House.

Lewis, C.S. 1980. *The Weight of Glory and Other Addresses. Revised and Expanded Edition. New York, NY:* MacMillan.

Lewis, C.S. 1967. *Christian Reflections.* Grand Rapids: William B. Eerdmans Publishing.

Lewontin, Richard. January 9, 1997. "Billions and Billions of Demons." *The New York Review of Books.*

Luskin, Casey. 2007. *"A Response to Dr. Dawkins 'The Information Challenge.'"* Evolution News and Views. www.discovery.org/a/4278. Accessed April, 2017.

Margulis, Lynn. February 3, 2006. Quoted in Darry Madden, UMass Scientist to Lead Debate on Evolutionary Theory, *Brattleboro (Vt.) Reformer.* www.

evolutionnews.org/2015/01/problem3rando/. Accessed February 2017.

Marks, Jonathan. 2003. *What it Means to Be 98% Chimpanzee: Apes, People, and Their Genes.* Los Angeles, CA: University of California Press.

Martin, Jobe. 2008. *The Evolution of a Creationist.* Rockwall, TX: Biblical Discipleship Publishers.

Mayr, Ernst. 1942. *Systematics and the Origin of Species.* Manhattan, NY: Columbia University Press.

Merriam-Webster Dictionary. 2016. *Definition of Chance.* Accessed November, 2016. http://www.merriam-webster.com/dictionary/chance.

Meyer, Stephen C. *The Signature in the Cell: DNA and the Evidence for Intelligent Design.* New York, NY: Harper Collins.

Meyer, Stephen C. Scott Minnich, Jonathan Moneymaker, Paul A. Nelson, and Ralph Seelke. 2007. *Explore Evolution: The Arguments For and Against Neo-Darwinism.* Melbourne and London: Hill House Publishers.

Miller, Kenneth R. 2003. *Answering the Biochemical Argument from Design.* Accessed January, 2017. www.millerandlevine.com/km/evol/design1/article.html.

Milton, Richard. 1997. *Shattering the Myths of Darwinism.* Rochester VT: Street Press.

Morris, Simon Conway. 2003. *Life's Solution: Inevitable Humans in a Lonely Universe.* Cambridge: Cambridge University Press.

Muggeridge, Malcolm. 1980. *The End of Christendom, But Not of Christ.* Grand Rapids: William B. Eerdmans Publishing Co.

Nagel, Thomas. 2012. *Mind and Cosmos: Why the Materialist Neo-Darwinian Conception of Nature is Almost Certainly False.* Oxford UK: Oxford University Press.

Obama, Barack. September 24, 2008. "News Feature: Q&A, US Election: Questioning the Candidates." *Nature*, International weekly journal of science. www.nature.com/news/2008/080924/full/455446a. html. Accessed March 2017.

Pascal, Blaise. A.J. Krailsheimer translator. 1995. *Pensees.* New York, NY: Penguin Putnam Inc.

Patterson, Colin. 1978. *Evolution.* Ithaca, NY: Cornell University Press.

Patterson, Colin. 1993. Talk, *American Museum of Natural History.* From a fax dated April 16, 1993. www.

talkorigins.org/faqs/patterson.html. Accessed March 2017.

Rana, Fazale and Hugh Ross. 2015. *Who Was Adam? A Creation Model Approach to the Origin of Humanity*, Second Expanded Edition. Covina, CA: RTB Press.

Rose, Michael quoted in Ian Sample. July 21, 2009. *Evolution: Charles Darwin was wrong about the tree of life.* The Guardian.Com. Accessed November, 2016. www.theguardian.com/science/2009/jan/21/charles-darwin-evolution-species-tree-life.

Sawyer, Robert. 2009. *Calculating God.* New York, NY: Tor Books.

Shapiro, James. September 16, 1996. Review of "Darwin's Black Box," by Michael Behe, *National Review.*

Spurgeon, Charles Haddon. 1855. *The Remembrance of Christ.* The New Park Street Pulpit, The Spurgeon Archive. www.spurgeon.org/sermons/0002.php. Accessed April, 2017.

Wikipedia. *Convergent Evolution.* Accessed March 18, 2013. http://en.wikipedia.org/wiki/Convergent_ evolution.

Yockey, Hubert. 1992. *Information Theory and Molecular Biology.* UK: Cambridge University Press.

PHOTO CREDITS

———— ∞∞∞ ————

229

Notes

Notes

Notes

Made in the USA
Columbia, SC
11 April 2018